Esther M Creery Dennas
55, Dennas Pk 875635

JASON
M Y   C H I L D

GW00599257

M A R T H A   V I T A L E

JASON

MY CHILD

JASON MY CHILD
Martha Vitale

OlivePress
2333 Main Street
Glastonbury, CT 06033
203.659.4393

FIRST EDITION
ISBN 0-9631200-3-4
Printed and bound in the United States of America

JASON
MY CHILD

MARTHA VITALE

DEDICATION

To Bethany, Bryan, MaryEllen, Sarah, and Ashley — five special blessings who continue to fill our hearts and our days with gladness.

TABLE OF **CONTENTS**

PREFACE

I can't imagine any of us who knew and loved Jason ever trying to describe him without focusing on his acceptance of God's having allowed his illness. His assurance came from a settled realization that the Lord knew what He was doing when the disease was first detected. His faith was indeed childlike: completely dependent upon someone else to do the planning and arranging, Someone who knew far more and was absolutely in total control of the whole situation. He lived with the hope that life would go on for him as normally as possible, but if it didn't, as he put it, "It's all in His hands."

He talked confidently of going to heaven, as though it were an upcoming trip he would be taking soon. He looked at things in a manner most unusual for a child. The window through which he saw life was not fogged by unreality and passing toys. A most engaging, lively little boy, he enjoyed all the typical childhood activities — having fun, going to school, playing with friends, reading good books — but there was also a seriousness about him that drew the attention of those around him. When asked to write a tribute to their friend, Jason's fifth grade classmates didn't remark on the four-wheeling adventures he loved; it was his kindness, sincere friendliness, thoughtfulness, care for others, and "his not being like other children" that they remembered.

Jason used the reality of his sickness to make others realize that having Christ as Savior is the only possession in life that we can take with us into eternity. I sat with him in his final moments, and watched his little ship slowly move away from this shore to another. It went safely across, with no long, stormy voyage, but was immediately "with Christ, which is far better." He was welcomed home by the One he had never seen, yet knew so well. The Savior Jason trusted as a young child was not only his Friend through life, but was also there to meet him on the other side.

Joey Procopio

INTRODUCTION

Every mother believes her child is special. In the first moments of life, something magical happens. From then on, a mother feels she is watching part of her heart perform outside of herself. Having given birth to seven children, I understand that each one is special. The feeling is the same regardless of the child's place in the family. This book is not an attempt to impress others with Jason's exceptional qualities. Its purpose is to present the remarkable way God comes in to meet our every need. Jason, in simple faith, bowed to the Lord's will and thus became an example to us all. His story is not one of tremendous sadness and defeat but an account of the triumph one can experience through trust in God.

Wes and I want to express our sincere gratitude to everyone who played a part in Jason's story. It was impossible to name each one in the pages of this book — that does not mean that anyone has been forgotten.

We owe a great deal to the medical personnel with whom we worked so closely for many years. Their unsurpassed compassion and support will long be remembered.

To our families, and the many Christian friends who treated us as family, we owe so much. We cannot imagine what this story would be like without their part in it.

To the people of New Hampshire and the Merrimac Valley, we owe our deep appreciation. The outflow of love and concern that came through the mail was incredible. Children drew pictures, wrote letters, and sent photographs and good luck charms to brighten Jason's days and warm our hearts. People we had never met took time to write letters to a little boy they read about in the papers. How could we ever thank everyone personally? We can only hope the message of thanks is transmitted clearly in the writing, because it will remain in our hearts eternally.

CHAPTER ONE

TIME STOPS

"It is leukemia."

Those were the words that froze time and stopped our world from turning. We were sitting in the offices of Dr. Truman, a specialist in Boston.

He had begun very graciously, "I told you earlier that what we were facing was most likely aplastic anemia or leukemia. Well, it is leukemia."

It was November 7, 1983 — a day seared into our memories for life. The doctor was speaking about our 4 1/2-yr.-old son, our Jason. Numbly, we nodded. This was really happening. No one was going to come in and say "There's been a mistake, Jason will be fine in a few days." He really had cancer. We were nodding in agreement because it was impossible to speak. With no real warning, our lives suddenly seemed to be turning upside down. We did not fully realize it at the time but we were about to enter a whole different world — a subculture with its own language, phrases, significant dates, heroes, villains and role-models.

It had all begun a few days before. The fiftieth anniversary of my beloved grandparents was coming up and my mother had planned a special dinner at a very quaint little restaurant in Connecticut. All my brothers and sisters would be there and it would be wonderful to be together to celebrate such a special occasion. That it was also the 6th wedding anniversary for Wes and me seemed insignificant compared to their 50th, yet it was precious to us. We were convinced the Lord had drawn us together and were thankful for the love and happiness we had shared. It was also a little overwhelming to think that in those six years we had three children — Jason, Bethany and Bryan. We weren't so sure we wanted to keep up that pace for the next six years... but we loved each of our children dearly.

The anniversary party was Saturday, November 5th, so we made plans to go to Connecticut on Saturday morning. My friend, Shawn, was going to baby-sit. Everything was set. Friday, Jason's color was strange. He was sitting on the kitchen table having his hair trimmed; wrinkling his little nose as the wisps of falling blond hair tickled his face. I noticed his face nearly matched the gold walls. Other strange things had been happening, too. He had complained of the light hurting his eyes and of his legs being too tired to walk. He had a physical when he started nursery school in September and every thing seemed normal. Why, just a few weeks later, was he looking so pale? I thought this might be serious and called the doctor. However, it was Friday afternoon and the office was busy. I was put on hold and apparently forgotten. I hung up and by the time I called again the office was closed. It wouldn't matter now if we waited until Monday morning. Once more, looking back, I am glad that things happened as they did or we would never have made it to the anniversary party.

When we arrived at my mother's in Connecticut she took one look at Jason and nearly fainted. She describes what she felt as a weakness behind her knees and a buzzing behind her ears. Being a nurse and seeing her grandson in that condition didn't give her any comfort.

She asked how he had been acting and said "Oh, honey, you get that child to a doctor as soon as you get home. With color like that the first thing you'll have to do is rule out leukemia."

We all just looked at each other. My sister, Mary Ellen, was upset with mom for saying such a thing. She thought that sounded ridiculous. I would have liked to think that sounded crazy but I knew my mother would not have said such a thing if she did not really suspect it was true. Some nurses are alarmists but my mother never was. She is realistic and usually when she suspected something when we were young she was right. There was nothing we could do about it until Monday so we went on with our plans. The evening was a success and Grammy and Grampy Flint had a good time. I had compiled a memory book for them of pictures and brief writings of incidents that we all remembered about them. They had a good time recalling Mary Ellen's giving Grammy a rubber snake, the dog and cat fighting, our grinding peanuts into peanut butter on her stone wall, etc. Amidst all the laughter and joy I could not shake the misgivings I was feeling about Jason's health. Leukemia?

Sunday night we returned home to New Hampshire. Wes called the pediatrician's office. The doctor on call listened as Wes explained all the symptoms puzzling us. There was nothing to be done then, but he asked us to meet our doctor in the office the following morning at nine. It sounded like a possible liver problem or hepatitis. We went to bed knowing that at least by the next day we would know what was wrong with our son.

We were fortunate at that time to have Wes's parents living next door. That would prove to be a tremendous help in the months ahead. On that unforgettable Monday morning, we were able to leave Bryan and Bethany with them and take Jason for his appointment.

Our doctor had been filled in and was expecting us. He was noticeably concerned when he saw Jason. He examined him and sent us across the street for blood work. That was Jason's first experience in what was to be a never-ending series of punctures and needles. He was very brave and I was amazed that he hardly whimpered. His big blue eyes solemnly studied the technicians as they drew blood from the inside of his arm. He was feeling very weak and not at all himself, yet he was easy to manage and the technicians marveled at the stamina of a four-year-old. We were proud of him. When that was completed we went back across the street to learn what they wanted us to do next. We were a bit surprised to hear and see our dear pediatrician.

He was quiet and shaken as he said, "Something is very wrong with his blood counts. I have gone ahead and called a very good doctor in Boston and he is waiting for you. Get there as soon as you can. I'm very, very sorry."

He hadn't told us what he felt was wrong but there was no way for him to be absolutely sure then. The specialist in Boston would decide. My heart really went out to him that day and to every doctor that has the dreadful task of telling parents of young children (and anyone else for that matter) that something serious is wrong with one they love. It certainly is not an easy job.

So we were on our way again still not knowing for sure what we were facing. In my heart I knew Jason had leukemia and that he was a very sick little boy.

I think I said that to Wes in the car because I remember his saying, "We just don't know. We'll have to wait and see. We know it's serious or we wouldn't be going to Boston but we'll just have to leave it in God's hands."

I knew that was true and always since I've loved him just a

little bit more for saying what he did. Somehow he always said the right thing to me, helping me to rely more on God and less on my own strength, something I had very little of at that moment.

Mass General's pediatric hematology/oncology clinic was on the 6th floor of what was then called the Ambulatory Care Center of Massachusetts General Hospital. That is the oldest hospital in New England, having treated its first patient in 1821. It is a massive labyrinthine hospital, part modern and part archaic, situated between the Charles River and Government Center. One would have thought William Ernest Henley had this facility in mind when he wrote:

"The hospital, gray, quiet, old
Where life and death like friendly chauffeurs meet."

The head of the clinic, Dr. Truman, was tall, distinguished and a true gentleman. We both liked him right away and felt instinctively that he knew what he was doing. His nurses, Sue and Monica, understood the confusion and fear we were feeling. As time went on we came to appreciate them as dedicated, caring professionals, who at the same time became almost part of our family. They entertained Jason while Dr. Truman spoke with us.

He explained that Jason would need a bone marrow aspiration and biopsy. A long thin needle would be inserted directly into the bone and a small amount of marrow fluid withdrawn (aspirated) for examination under a microscope. The biopsy would involve removal of a small core of bone. From the information we already had, Dr. Truman felt that we were dealing with either aplastic anemia or leukemia. They both sounded bad. I remember asking "If given a choice, which one should we choose?"

The doctor said, "Well, as strange as it may seem, it is easier to treat leukemia."

So, incredible as it now sounds, I began to silently pray that my little boy had leukemia!

While we were waiting for the test results it was suggested

that we get some lunch and walk around a bit. There was a lot to grasp and maybe a change of scenery would help. On the way to the elevator we passed a phone. We knew by now everyone at home must surely be wondering where we were, so Wes called his mother and had the awful job of telling her what we were facing. It was a difficult call to make and, no doubt, to receive.

Bad news usually travels fast and that day was no exception. By the time we returned to the office Wes's dad and two very special friends — Fred Hill and his daughter, Jacki Smith — were waiting for us.

Uncle Fred ran his fingers through his snow white hair, smiled gently and asked, "So how's my buddy ole pal?

"Uncle Fred" had left a sick bed and Jacki four children to be with us. It is something I will never forget. At such a difficult hour it was so reassuring to have loved ones rally round and offer support. Just knowing we were not alone meant so much. Dad was able to joke with Jason and to get his mind off his troubles. Having his Grampy there made things a little better even though he was feeling tired and afraid.

When the time came to go in and hear the verdict, nothing could make things better for us. I felt that we were awaiting a sentence in court. In a way we were, because nothing would ever be quite the same again. While our minds were whirling we went along as if nothing were wrong. What else was there to do? Jason needed the security of strong parents and, by the grace of God, that was what he was going to get no matter how hard it was to act "normal." The staff was kind enough to include all in the discussion that followed. Usually Dr. Truman addresses just the parents but that day there were five of us.

And so, with an ominous sense of foreboding, we heard his diagnosis. When words did come we asked what the next steps were and what chance Jason had of recovering. Suddenly there were so many questions and so much to learn. A chemotherapy protocol —

a program of drugs and dosages — would be randomly selected by computer because two different ones were being tried nationwide. Blood transfusions were needed, as well as a spinal tap to see if the disease had infiltrated the spinal fluid. Tomorrow would be another day and Jason had been through enough for one day. Tomorrow we would also find out more about the type of leukemia we were treating and which risk group he was in. There would be tomorrow...yet it was no longer a day to look forward to.

Amid all our almost instantaneous fears and trepidation, God granted us a peace and a calm acceptance of the situation that I marvel at today. We did not lash out in anger or go to pieces. We knew that God would do what was best for Jason and would see that we had the necessary strength to endure whatever lay ahead. I cannot imagine going through that day, and the many following, without that assurance. Knowing that there was a God who held our breath in his hand, numbered the hairs of our heads, and was ready to help us was a tremendous comfort. But then, sitting in that doctor's office, it was difficult to imagine getting up and continuing daily life. There were questions from Dad and Uncle Fred as a few tears ran silently down Jacki's cheeks. This was overwhelming for us all. When it seemed there was nothing left to do but leave, Uncle Fred suggested we pray. Although they were invited to stay, the staff left quickly and Uncle Fred commended Jason and us, his parents, into the Lord's hands. He knew our future was uncertain and that we would need God's help on a moment-by-moment basis. How true!

Where had this invader come from? Had Jason been fine one day and leukemic the next? Our minds were filled with questions, some of which would never be answered. The cause of leukemia is not known. Some feel it starts with a virus, while others think that it has more to do with the immune system's malfunctioning. For whatever reason, Jason's bone marrow was not behaving correctly. We had always thought leukemia was "cancer of the blood."

This is not an accurate description. The bone marrow produces all the blood cells for the body. There are white cells, red cells, and platelets. Jason's marrow had something extra. There were abnormal cells present called "blasts." While the red cells were carrying oxygen, the white cells fighting infection, and the platelets controlling bleeding, these blasts were doing nothing but overcrowding the marrow. In such overcrowded conditions it is impossible for the good cells to work properly. Because red cells were lacking, Jason was anemic, in danger of bleeding and susceptible to infection. We did not understand all of this that first day in the office. It would take time for all that we had been told to sink in.

It was dark when we left the hospital and as we traveled rather quietly up the highway Jason looked out at all the lights. "Do people die from leukemia? It's really bad, isn't it?"

It would have been so easy to lie to him. Saying "Oh no, it's not that bad" sounded so much better than being honest. Yet how could we lie only to have him find out later on?

"Yes, some people do die with this disease but many get better and go right back to a normal life."

He thought about this for a minute and said, "Well, that's okay, God will take care of me and do whatever He wants."

The faith of a child was a marvel to witness. He was perfectly content to leave it with the Lord. How much we could learn from him!

Suddenly Jason recognized we were on Route 1.

"Let's go see Joey," he practically yelled.

Joe Procopio was a close friend who was the best man at our wedding and had later married my cousin Jan. Jason was crazy about him. It seemed only natural that, after the kind of day he had put in, he would want to see him. Although we were anxious to get home, we decided to stop by his place, a few minutes from the highway. As Joe opened the door he was very surprised to see us. He gathered Jason up for a hug. Living in New Hampshire, we did not drop in

10

often. He was more puzzled to see that only Jason was with us.

We explained where we had been and told him, "Jason has leukemia."

Poor Joe! Putting myself in his place now, I think we were not very tactful in telling him. Perhaps there is no right way to deliver bad news. His smiles faded quickly and he paled as Jason told him about the tests he had. Jason seemed glad to be able to tell someone special just how he felt and how brave he had tried to be. Although the visit was very short it seemed to make going home easier because we were slowly getting used to the idea as we talked about it.

Home. It is usually the most welcome of sights, a place to relax, to kick off your shoes and unwind. This time my feet felt like lead weights as I walked toward the door. Once inside I felt better. The other children had missed us and wanted to hug Jason.

Bethany, her golden ponytails flying, came skipping over to hug her brother. She backed away only slightly to ask, "Are you okay?"

Bryan smiled and crawled over to us, happy we were home again. His blue eyes sparkled and he giggled at Jason.

Yes, things were more normal here. Wes's sister, Faith, was there with her baby and, from the look of things, both she and Mom had put in a very upsetting day as well. Their eyes were red and teary and we could read the heartache on their faces. Truly, a family suffers together just as it rejoices together. There was no rejoicing now, only confusion and uncertainty. The phone kept ringing, connecting us with family and friends wanting to comfort and offer their help in whatever capacity they could. The pain was real for them, too. If the callers lived far away, they felt guilty because they couldn't help. If they worked, that made it difficult to pitch in. Everyone felt so helpless. There was one thing that everyone could do, though, and that was to pray for all of us. The power of prayer is truly amazing and we could actually feel the strength it brought.

It meant so much to hear the concern and to know that so many friends were there for us. Without them it would have been a lonely time. As I was thinking along these lines, the door bell rang and in walked Uncle Joe and Aunt Fran (Joey's parents). They had taken the time, on a chilly November evening, to drive for an hour just to let us know of their concern. Things like that are not forgotten. The support gained from the unselfish help of friends carried us over many rough times.

CHAPTER TWO

REALITIES

November 8th Jason began his chemotherapy. We are thankful for the medicines presently available– not too long ago we would have gone home to watch our son die. Now, by giving a series of different drugs at different times for varied time periods many types of leukemia can be cured. We learned that Jason had Acute Lymphocytic Leukemia (ALL), which is the most common of the childhood leukemias. He was also in the low risk category because it was felt that there had been an early diagnosis and his blood counts could have been much worse. These were good signs and something to be thankful for.

He was put on a three year protocol: the first five months would be intensive chemotherapy, followed by a rigorous mainte-nance program. It was the doctor's opinion that everything would

go smoothly for us. Jason's chances for a complete recovery were es-
timated at 75%. This was a relief, in a way, because suddenly everything looked a little brighter. It was easier to put him through this
treatment if it meant he would get better. Jason had his spinal tap
and the fluid was clear, which meant the disease was contained in
the bone marrow. This was another good sign. The blood transfusions followed and lasted all day. Then he had his first dose of the
drug vincristine. We were given papers explaining what each drug
was for and what side effects to expect. Vincristine would cause
bone pain and hair loss. That was an idea to get used to — a four
year old with no hair. Looking back I laugh at myself for thinking
that was such a big thing! Some of the other drugs that he would be
given might cause cardiac irregularities, kidney and liver dysfunc-
tion, brain damage and severe allergic reactions.

The next few days went fairly smoothly. Jason was feeling
happier and looked healthy from the new blood. Where there were
once pale, yellowish cheeks, rosy ones returned. The medicine
seemed to be doing its job. But by the weekend things were no
longer calm. We started to see some of those side effects we had
read about. Jason's mouth was burning and his jaw hurt. He was
very constipated and unhappy.

We would learn that there were going to be good days and
bad days, and often very bad days; days when he wouldn't even be
able to swallow his saliva because of mouth sores, or to eat because
of extended periods of vomiting. This was all new to us. We weren't
sure what to expect. Months of chemotherapy were ahead, for this
was just the start of a three-year protocol.

Some days I thought I would never make it if the entire time
was to be like the first few weeks. The prednisone made Jason rav-
enously hungry. He would eat three breakfasts, the first usually in
the wee hours of dawn while the rest of us slept. His moods were
sometimes black. The slightest thing would send him into orbit. On
the other hand, something only mildly funny would trigger fits of

uncontrollable laughter. This was difficult to deal with, because I knew this behavior was not his fault. I tried to be patient, but could not just allow him to take advantage of his brother and sister or get whatever he wanted just because he was ill. If the Lord spared him and he did get well then he would be impossible to live with!

There were difficult days at home, and difficult days at the hospital. Jason's attitude towards chemo was generally fine. He prided himself on being the bravest one there and rarely shed a tear when having intravenous inserted or a bone marrow aspiration or spinal tap. We usually had a very easy time with him and I felt sorry for the mother who had to stand there helplessly and listen to her little one scream. In a manner that would characterize his entire illness, Jason was making this very easy for us by the way he handled it himself. But when veins would not cooperate and repeated sticking was needed, Jason was transformed into a frustrated and irritable little boy.

"You can't do this! You're never going to get it!" he'd accuse Sue, his ordinarily beloved nurse.

But after the ordeal was over, he'd apologize and hug her, and everything would be fine. These episodes were necessary reminders to Wes and me that he was, after all, just a little boy. He, like all the children we were meeting on our hospital visits, was experiencing something that should not be a part of childhood. Our circumstances were sharpening our senses to the pain others around us lived with. There was always something to make me thankful for my situation as I realized how much others were suffering. There was the family that had a child with both Down Syndrome and leukemia, and the parents whose only child had been stricken. I was constantly discovering someone worse off — and this awareness became such a part of my way of dealing with our situation that my sister-in-law said my motto was "It could be worse."

There was so much sadness, yet most of the time I hardly thought of being sad. Children would come in with pictures they had colored, or cookies and donuts for the staff. Of course there were the little ones who came in crying, continued crying the entire time they were there, and left crying. It was not that the place was particularly sad in itself; it was when we returned home and thought about the day and everyone we had seen that the helpless, aching feelings would come.

We made special friends, though, that we will never forget. The doctors and nurses became extensions of our family. Monica had been Dr. Truman's nurse for many years. To the children, she was like a grandmother with her loving and tender ways. Sue was a bubbly blond in her early 30's. She would laugh and joke with the kids and was usually hugging one of them. Dr. Truman was kind and gentle, very distinguished, yet not aloof. He loved his patients and was loved in return. Dr. Ferguson was a new young doctor when we first met. He added a lot to the clinic with his dry wit. He liked to see the bright side of life and helped us do the same.

When Jason began going every day for treatment he met Lauren, a sweet little redhead, who, at eleven, had been coming for three years already and had recently relapsed. Outgoing and friendly, she was quite grown up for her age and Jason was very impressed with her. She told us, in a matter-of-fact tone of voice, that "they" were trying to get her into remission again. This was new to us, as we had yet to reach one remission, and the thought of doing it repeatedly made me shudder. Her parents took everything calmly as well. Lauren was their youngest child and had been born when they were in their forties. At an age in life when parents are enjoying the freedom of grown children, they were spending most of their time at a hospital.

Lauren and Jason helped each other to be brave. They encouraged one another when a spinal tap was painful or a vein was hard to find. It was extremely helpful to have someone who understood how a bone marrow aspiration felt and how certain drugs burned. We parents could only try to help but what did we know about the world of tubes and needles?

The purpose for all the chemotherapy was to reach a remission. This is when the disease lies dormant and does not show up in tests. It could return if the drugs were immediately removed but eventually the patient can be weaned from his medication and, hopefully, the disease does not recur. If Jason could obtain a remission within four weeks everyone would be happy.

At the end of the third week Dr. Truman did another bone marrow aspiration. He was pleased to tell us that Jason was already in remission. We were thrilled! This was better than we had expected and Jason was indeed sailing along. We were concerned about sending him back to nursery school and felt he would be more protected from germs, etc. at home. However, the doctor felt that he needed the normalcy of school and the activity it provided so we decided to send him once he was feeling up to it, maybe after the holidays.

It was during the Christmas break that the most important event in Jason's life occurred. Jason had always shown a deep interest in spiritual things. He seemed to grasp and understand what many children (and adults) do not. Now that he was so seriously ill this interest only increased. So often he would be the one to remind us that God was in control and would do what was best for us all. We were so thankful that Jason was learning the Bible as we read it to him and during his regular attendance at Sunday school. At a very young age he knew of his need to accept the Lord Jesus Christ as his Savior. He understood that he had been born a sinner and needed forgiveness and salvation.

On Christmas morning Wes was having a discussion with my thirteen-year-old brother, Peter, about the importance of being saved — having one's sins forgiven. As they lay on the couch chatting Jason was listening to every word. He was drinking in the simple message of salvation and finally interrupted.

"Daddy, can *I* get saved? I'd like to get saved now."

19

Wes was surprised, but thrilled. He had not been paying attention to this little guy next to him. Wes quoted Isaiah 53:5-6: *"But He was wounded for our transgressions, He was bruised for our iniquities, the chastisement of our peace was upon Him and with His stripes we are healed. All we like sheep have gone astray, we have turned every one to his own way and the Lord hath laid on Him the iniquity of us all."*

He continued quoting other scriptures to him. Jason knew most of them by heart. Among them was John 3:16: *"For God so loved the world that He gave His only begotten Son, that whosoever believeth in Him should not perish but have everlasting life."*

Jason listened as his Dad told him that the Lord said *"Him that cometh to Me I will in no wise cast out."* Wes asked him if he knew what that meant.

Without answering, Jason said, "I'm going to ask Him to save me right now." He climbed off the couch and knelt beside it there in the basement. He did not speak out loud but got up, eyes shining and said, "Now I know that I'm saved."

Initially I was doubtful that a child who was so young could understand an issue so momentous. Having been saved at fifteen myself I wondered how this little one, a few months shy of five, had been able to grasp salvation. However, the Lord said in Matthew 18:3, *"Except ye be converted, and become as little children, ye shall not enter into the kingdom of heaven."* Salvation is not complex and adults must become childlike to receive it. As the years unfolded we witnessed a reality and maturity in Jason that we could never have dreamed of that Christmas morning.

When the holidays were over, Jason was feeling so much better that he returned to school. His teachers were delighted with the Jason that returned. He had personality and energy! To my astonishment, they had known him as a shy, quiet and rather disinterested child. Now, thanks to the chemotherapy, his energy level was back to normal and he was alert, involved and outgoing — the way we'd always known him. They were thrilled to discover the real Jason.

Over the next few months, Jason did miss quite a bit of school. But he loved going. School was a welcome change from the world of needles, treatments and disease, and gave him a sense of normalcy.

While he seemed to be doing well, we were forced to realistically face the idea that something could go wrong and we might yet lose him. We were told to get used to the idea of having two children rather than three because this disease was sneaky at best and there were no guarantees. Bethany and Bryan were such a delight to us but the prospect of losing Jason was, nonetheless, hard to contemplate. When, in a short time, we learned that we were going to have another child, we were convinced that this was a blessing from God. This became even more obvious later on. Never had we felt so aware of His hand in our lives and He seemed to give us a sense of quiet strength as things returned more and more to normal, every-day life.

While things progressed for Jason, they regressed for Lauren. Late in the spring we saw her. She came in to chat with Jason while waiting to be examined. She offered us red licorice and very calmly said she had relapsed again. My heart ached for her. The nurses were talking with her mother about bone marrow transplant. I wasn't sure what this was, exactly, but knew enough to realize that she needed another remission first. That remission never came.

Our next appointments did not coincide, as Jason was not going very often, but on one of his visits Lauren was there. She talked to Jason and hugged the staff as she left. Perhaps she knew she would not be back. The next day we received word that Lauren had died at home. We told Jason very gently and he cried the kind of tears one cries at the loss of a special friend.

He decided death was unfair because "I never saw her for the last time." Wes explained that he had seen her just the other day.

"But I didn't know it was the last time," he cried.

How true! We never know when the last time has come. So, one warm evening in the summer of 1984 we traveled the 80 miles to Lauren's wake. Jason had insisted on coming, though I wasn't totally convinced this was such a good idea. His logic was that he needed to say good-bye. The church was crowded and a long line of people stretched from the building through the parking lot. When we reached the door we discovered that the line wound up three flights of stairs as well. As we waited, Jason was nervous but determined. He was ready to deal with this. Before long the casket came into view. We could see it was closed and I was silently grateful for not having to look down into that lively little face now stilled.

As our turn came Lauren's father spotted Jason, swept him up into his arms and sobbed softly as he hugged him over and over. Her mother was deeply touched that Jason had been so anxious to come. We looked at her schoolmates' drawings hanging behind the casket and talked about Lauren, whose freckled face smiled at us from a photograph on the coffin. We longed to see her, vibrant and enthusiastic, bouncing into the doctor's office again, but that would never be. For Lauren, there would be no more needles and no more chemotherapy. We could not wish her back. We visited her home later that night and Jason saw her room and her stuffed animals. In some way this put his young mind at ease. He was unscathed by the experience and would remember Lauren alive and smiling, because that was how he saw her, even this, the very last time.

CHAPTER THREE

MARYELLEN

It was encouraging to see Jason looking so well. He was able to run and play like all the other children. He was leading a normal life and experiencing the usual mishaps, too. With the five months behind him he was enjoying summer, just having fun, when he stepped on a rusty nail. He had been riding his tricycle and skidded to a stop right on the nail. The howling could have been heard all over the neighborhood!

As I carried him to the house he shrieked, "Now I'm really going to die!"

Apparently all our well-intentioned warnings — "Please be careful! Don't take chances! We don't want you to get an infection!" had made more of an impression than we realized. We soaked his foot and called Boston and his panic passed when he learned that a tetanus shot would make him as good as new. Not many weeks later he didn't notice that his finger was in the car door when he slammed it shut. Once again the neighborhood was filled with howling. This time, however, he knew it wasn't life-threatening, just painful. Not only had he removed the finger nail, he had broken his finger!

But other than the normal childhood accidents, Jason enjoyed a healthy summer. We visited aunts and uncles in Pennsylvania, went to the beach, had picnics and enjoyed a fun New England summer. When it was over and time for school again we had collected many happy memories.

This school year would be different as Jason would be going to kindergarten every morning rather than having three mornings of nursery school. He was looking forward to it and frequently asked me to read the class list so he could see which children he knew from the previous year. Friends were important to a five-year-old. It meant a lot to know who liked you and whom you liked. Once school started he would come home and decorate the refrigerator with his projects. Bethany usually added hers as she was now in nursery school. Kindergarten was fun and Jason rarely missed a day. The appointments in Boston were once every two weeks now and could easily be scheduled in the afternoon.

He made lots of friends and usually came home happy. However, the medication he was on caused his body to swell and there were days when his feelings were hurt by those who called him names because of his appearance. He would come home very quiet and eventually the truth would come out that some school child had called him "chubby cheeks" or "fatty." There was no way to protect him from such incidents. These five-year-olds were not always trying to be mean. They didn't think before they spoke and simply said whatever came into their heads.

I explained all this to Jason as gently as I could. I suggested he tell the class why he looked like that and he thought that was a good idea. A few days later he came home and said he had talked to the children and they "said they were sorry and were real nice to me." On the whole, his classmates were very understanding. He was often invited to their homes to play and he loved to educate their parents about leukemia. Many of them didn't know he had it and couldn't believe he was so ill because he certainly didn't act it. I'd frequently hear them remark "how bright" or "how amazing" he was as he told them about his leukemia. Never once did he feel cheated out of a normal childhood or ask why he had to be the one to be sick. Instead, he would talk about God's having given him this disease because He knew he could handle it and would be able to trust Him. Not too many adults would have that outlook!

Along with enjoying kindergarten, Jason was anxiously awaiting his new brother or sister. Actually he had decided that this baby had to be a girl.

"We already have two boys and a mommy and daddy but only one girl and it won't be fair to have four boys but only two girls."

Just when October was ending in a flurry of leaves and neighborhood goblins the score was evened; MaryEllen was born. Dark hair and deep blue eyes, she was beautiful. Everything about her birth was uncomplicated and easy and I felt wonderful. There is something so precious about a new life.

Wes was happy that she was here but was having a hard time coping with a sense of "numbness." He was proud and thankful for another healthy daughter but something was different this time. Later we realized that he had been expecting a replacement for Jason and this tiny little bundle was not Jason. She was perfect but there was no way to have a "spare" Jason should something happen to the first. When Wes understood all of this the numbness disappeared and he fell in love with this darling little girl God had given us. She was the most content of all our babies, so much so that she almost starved herself. The pressures I was under left me unable to nurse well and at four weeks of age she was a pound under her birth weight. Formula took care of that and she discovered eating wasn't such a waste of time after all. She was a wonderful blessing for us all to enjoy.

The rest of the school year progressed well. Actually it seemed to fly by. With a new baby, a two-year-old, plus two in school who needed transporting, life was busy. It is difficult to recall events from those months. I must have been too tired to function. Before we knew it we were again thrust into summer with the ending of school in June of 1985.

It had been a good year for Jason. At six he looked no different from any of his healthy friends. Yet something did not seem quite right. He was easily agitated and cross. I complained to my mother that he acted like he was on prednisone even though he wasn't. He had a visit coming up with Dr. Truman and I wanted to be sure to tell him about it.

A few nights later when I went up to bed I found Jason walking around. When I questioned him he said his leg hurt. He went back to bed with no fuss so I assumed he had a cramp. During the night he came into our room complaining of pain in his chest. This was very strange. He tried to settle down in our bed but ended up again pacing the floor. It was about four A.M. by now. We knew it was too early to call the doctor so we waited until six and then tried to reach Dr. Truman at his home.

He returned the call promptly and said he had been sitting reading. He had awakened early and sensed that a patient was in trouble. He had chosen to read while waiting for the phone to ring. Since I had promised to baby-sit my sister-in-law Faith's two-year-old, Wes would have to go to Boston alone. At the last minute he decided to swing by his parents' house and his dad went with him. I reassured Faith when she dropped off the baby that everything would probably be fine, and she and her husband left. They had not gone too far when they decided to turn around just in case Jason wasn't okay. They came back and Faith stayed with me until we had some news.

Finally Wes called to say the doctor thought it might be shingles because he had noticed three or four dots on Jason's left shoulder. He wanted to do a bone marrow just to eliminate the possibility of a relapse.

"Wes, he doesn't have shingles!" I blurted out. " He brushed against a thorn bush. Those dots are just the scars left from the scratch."

A bone marrow! Jason absolutely hated that! I had to get there. Racing down I-93 towards Boston, desperate to cover those 50 miles, I prayed, "Lord, get me there in time. Jason needs me!" My mind flashed back to a day years before when I had sped along another highway to Boston. It was my father doing the driving. My sister, Mary Ellen, was in the hospital there and we were hurrying to meet a specialist. Suddenly I ached for my father. He had divorced my mother several years before and we rarely kept in touch. If only he were here now. Right out loud, all alone in the car, I begged God to reach him and bring him back. It was probably for selfish reasons that I prayed as I did that day. It would have been so reassuring to have "my Daddy" there making everything all right as he did when I was a little girl. Immediately I realized I was not alone and told my Heavenly Father I was sorry for being so unappreciative of His presence and His desire to strengthen me. With these thoughts I began to calm down as the long ride finally came to an end. Within minutes I was running up the hallway to my son.

CHAPTER **FOUR**

BAD NEWS

The morning had been rough on everyone. Jason had already had the bone marrow and was whimpering. Dad and Wes looked like they had been through the mill. Wes was drained, but Dad seemed to be talking endlessly about anything that came into his mind. No one needed to ask him if he were nervous! I had only been there for a few minutes when Wes and I were called into Dr. Truman's office.

The doctor sighed and leaned back in his chair, looking weary and disturbed. "I'm afraid I have some bad news," he said. "The leukemia is back. Unfortunately, the disease is stronger than the chemicals trying to combat it. Chemotherapy is not going to work. We can most likely obtain another remission but we cannot hold it. There will be more relapses and possibly more remissions, but each will be shorter than the one before. Eventually there will be no further remission."

We looked at each other, then back at Dr. Truman.

"So now what do we do?"

"Bone marrow transplant," he replied.

I remembered Lauren telling us that's what she was waiting for. Now it was Jason! What was it? The doctor explained that first Jason would have to be brought back into remission. Then a compatible donor would have to be found. Jason's bone marrow would then be treated with chemotherapy and, possibly, with radiation to destroy it. Next, the healthy marrow from the donor would be put into his system (transfused) where it would multiply and completely replace his dead marrow. It sounded simple enough.

"What are the chances of success?"

"Not much better than 30%-40%."

"What are Jason's long term chances without it?"

"Zero."

What choice did we have? None!

"Where do we find a donor?"

"Hopefully, in one of his siblings."

This could affect Bethany, Bryan, or MaryEllen! What would they have to be put through? Was there risk for them? I was terribly confused! I had always feared a relapse and, now that it had occurred, it introduced a whole new set of problems and, at the moment, somewhat of a numbness.

There wasn't much to be said at that point. We left, with our new goal to get Jason back into remission. I didn't want to face what I knew lay ahead; there would be more chemotherapy, more sickness, more moodiness, and more uncertainty. But with all my numbness and confusion, there was an awareness that, in spite of all the unknowns, there would be more grace and more strength from God, our "very present help in trouble."

I knew that the Lord would continue to help me to accept,

realistically, what was happening, do what needed to be done, and at the same time leave the whole situation with Him. I felt weary and weak, but not let down. I was prepared to go on knowing that this time, too, God would supply added strength and comfort. We had come this far and God was certainly able to do more than we could ask or think. We knew His will would be done. In my opinion, it was wrong to expect that God had to heal our son. If He chose not to, for reasons known only to Him, there would be no room for bitterness because God hadn't done what I thought He should. The best thing to do was to *really* leave it with Him and pray for the courage to accept whatever happened.

This was like starting all over again, with a stronger sense of urgency. If Jason did not reach a second remission, it was the beginning of the end. If he did reach remission and went on to have a bone marrow transplant, he still might not survive. It was difficult to know where to begin. I felt a tremendous need to hurry everything up. Unfortunately, nothing could be hurried, for every step would hinge on the results of the previous steps.

First, stronger chemotherapy would be administered for four weeks with the hope of achieving remission. Then we would have to find out which sibling, if any, would make a suitable donor. That would take more time. We would also need to find a hospital that would take Jason. We decided to investigate possible hospitals while we were waiting for remission, so that when the time came to act we would know which one to contact.

Wes did most of this research and was very surprised to find that, on the whole, hospitals were not all that concerned with our son's welfare. Money seemed more important than saving a six-year-old's life. Naturally, we had a difficult time accepting that. One institution wanted $100,000.00 on admission and another wanted $150,000.00. It was incredible!

When we asked whether we would be refused treatment if we did not have that amount available, our question was ignored.

Instead, the conversation was turned to a discussion on long waiting lists and limited beds.

When Jason first came down with leukemia we did not have medical insurance. Wes had been in business for himself for a short time and could not afford it. This really bothered me for a long time. We had always had excellent health coverage before. Why would the Lord allow Jason to get sick then? I knew God made no mistakes. It just seemed like it would have been so much easier without the burden of paying thousands and thousands of dollars to hospitals. I expressed these feelings to a friend who responded that maybe it was possible to be so insured that there was no room for God to work. I thought about that a lot and finally decided that it was true. Where is the need for God to provide and perform miracles if everything is taken care of by insurance? While I am *not* saying that insurance is wrong, I *am* saying that God was able, in our circumstances, to teach us a lot more about faith and trust than we might otherwise have learned.

While we investigated hospitals we also inquired about statistics for survival and for cure, etc. Wes was starting to wonder whether the transplant was too risky to try. I seconded his questions to some degree, but not to the point that I was ready to forego the transplant. I had the "advantage" of being at the hospital regularly and watching the children who went from one relapse to the next, growing weaker all the time and definitely not living a normal life. Wes thought that we could spend a quality year, or whatever time we had together, until Jason finally left us.

I realized there was no such thing as "quality time" when most of it would be spent in treatment and weakness. We knew that as Jason's parents we had to know that we had done everything there was to do and had exhausted every possibility before we said no to a suggested treatment. This was our personal feeling. Of parents that feel otherwise, I am not critical. There are very real threats to transplants and we faced the fact that we might be signing Jason's death warrant by agreeing to it. However, we felt that without it death would eventually come anyway.

While Wes tried to find a solution to the hospital situation, many of our friends were working hard at this same task. They were calling every conceivable organization to inquire about financial aid. No one could answer their questions in the way they had hoped. Referrals to other agencies and apologies for not being able to do anything were the standard replies. It was this exhausting and depressing attempt to be helpful that prompted them to call Washington, D.C. There must be some way to save Jason, even if it meant going to the President.

All this was being done without our involvement, so we were very surprised when a special phone call came one night.

Wes answered the phone and after he said, "Yes, I'll hold," he covered the phone and told me, with a look of total shock, "It's the White House!"

I was stunned, impatient for him to finish his conversation and fill me in. It was a Mr. Batton, one of the President's aides, who was calling to get all the details of our situation. After Wes had explained why we weren't able to pay for Jason's transplant, and what the hospitals were requiring, Mr. Batton was indignant.

"This is America, and we don't let six-year-olds die because they can't afford an operation! You relax and take care of your family. I'll notify the necessary offices, and we'll get this taken care of!"

Needless to say, this call left us excited and hopeful that things might come together after all! Earlier that evening, Wes had mentioned to his mother that running into so many dead ends was getting disheartening. His mother reminded him not to stop trusting that God would take care of things. When the call came, we could hardly believe that Washington would concern itself with our family!

When we had time to really think about it all we were almost ashamed. Just because the President called we had felt relief!

Wasn't the Lord on our side as well? Hadn't He, infinitely greater than any man, been concerned about our family all along? And doesn't His power far surpass any ability, even that of the President of this great country? We had been looking at things only from the human side. But God was going to show us that He could work this out apart altogether from the President and independent of all our efforts.

The White House call attracted the attention of the news media and Jason began to be very popular in the papers. This press coverage led to a special relationship with reporter Barbie Walsh, who became like one of the family during Jason's long illness. With all the media attention, many people became avid followers of his progress. The letters that came from these new friends boosted him through the frequent ups and downs of treatment. One of the first letters was from a man named Bob:

"Hi Jason!

I read about you in the paper tonight and I want to thank you and your mom and dad for all the nice things you all said. It made me feel real good. It still does! Just like your dad, Jason, I am also proud to be an American and I am glad the President is helping. I want to help too.

So I have enclosed a few dollars for you to spend for whatever you want. Please stay brave — I'm very, very proud of you and I am going to pray with my family and friends for you, to ask God to help you all be brave. Oh, by the way, I have a little Cocker Spaniel named Sasha that sure would like to see you someday, so we will be looking forward to seeing you. Remember, stay brave.

From a friend you haven't met yet,
Bob"

The support from the area was amazing. Children sent the contents of their piggy banks. Sweet, elderly folks sent all kinds of good-luck charms and kind letters with checks enclosed. Lists for thank you notes were longer every day and a growing warmth was felt in spite of the problems I knew would not go away.

CHAPTER FIVE

HELP

Jason was an outgoing child. People were attracted to his calm acceptance of a life-threatening illness and were intrigued by his trust in God. He knew what he was facing to some degree but much of it was difficult for us to explain since we as well were unsure what it would be like. He talked to everyone, though, about his feelings.

To Bethany he said, "It's okay if God wants me to die now."

They discussed heaven and the streets of gold. Bethany wasn't sure if she really believed that heaven had such streets, but Jason convinced her that if the Bible said so, it was true. They spoke of the ones they knew that were in heaven. Jason said he would see his great grandparents as well as Connie, Uncle Pat and Carl. These dear friends had died recently and it was easy for him to relate to their being in heaven because he remembered them alive.

Death was not discussed with fear, though lumps rose in our throats. It all was very simple to Jason. He told Barbie, the reporter, that he was not afraid of dying.

"I don't worry about it. I pretend I am a normal person. I pretend I'm just fine, that I don't have a disease. And nobody would ever know except for the holes in me."

Those holes were from chemotherapy that he was getting three days a week. He told of being brave and not crying when getting his shots. He was anxious to get it over with because he felt that I was upset and never really happy anymore. He worried about his brother and sisters having to be tested as possible donors. He wondered whether we would forget him if he died. That he was only six while dealing with all of this amazes me even now.

While we were groping for answers to his questions and trying to carry on as usual, the fund for his operation was growing. Local folks were planning fund-raisers in the form of Fun Days at the downtown park, balloon rides, bowl-athons, walk-athons, etc. We were amazed that everyone would care so much. Certainly it is easy to feel sorry for a family in a crisis, but these people were running errands, selling T-shirts, playing Superman, turning green to become the Hulk in a dunk tank, and painting dozens of faces with hearts and balloons. The list goes on and on. The K-Mart Corporation became interested in helping raise money in early August. This became a huge effort in its stores throughout the area and would eventually result in over $37,000.00 being raised for Jason's benefit. It was an awesome task and the effort put forth on our account was most touching.

We were seeing a side of people that many will never see. Some reporters said that our story was popular partially for this reason. In a world where no one seems trustworthy, crimes are committed around the clock, and evil abounds, we saw people giving freely of their time and money to help a six-year-old many of them would never meet. It was also our privilege, by way of the media, to tell thousands that our strength came from above and that we firmly believed God would do what was best for us all. There were times when much of what we said was never printed. Apparently faith in a living God and reliance on His will are not popular topics and don't sell papers. We answered the questions they asked and tried to keep our household running smoothly as meals were interrupted and routine in general was turned into chaos.

While every effort was being made to raise money we were running into problems with the State of New Hampshire. The Federal Government had promised to match state funds, but in fact, we would never receive a dime from either Washington or New Hampshire. When we applied to the state for medical aid we were refused because we provided Jason a stable home life. If one parent were absent from the home or one parent were unable to provide support or care, the story would have been different. But there was no aid available for happily married couples. We were horrified! It seemed so incredible that this was the reasoning behind the refusal! The media shared our sense of outrage. Papers carried the headline "STATE SAYS ITS RULES FORBID HELPING BOY" and accounts of New Hampshire's position began appearing. The clamor increased as the public became aware of the situation. There's no doubt in my mind that God's grace to us increased as well. What other reason can I give for my ability to courteously thank the women who called telling me to divorce Wes and set up a separate residence? How ridiculous! Patience with such advice would certainly not have been my natural reaction! Such well-meaning people thought they were helping and I treated them as if they were, but divorce? That was unthinkable!

As that August of 1985 began, Jason was once again in remission. It had taken exactly a month. We were so relieved, because everything else hinged on this! Next, we needed to find a donor. This was to be a sibling, and even with three to choose from, the chances, statistically, were not great. But I had a feeling that the baby, MaryEllen, would be the one. The events surrounding her birth had seemed to mean something, and this could be the answer.

One afternoon in early August we all went to have blood drawn at Mass General. This identification procedure is known as human lymphocyte antigen typing, or HLA. The little ones were nervous as technicians drew 20 cc's from their arms (30 cc's equals about 1 ounce). The baby gave 15 cc's and Wes, Jason and myself, 75 cc's. These tubes seemed enormous to Jason as he was used to much smaller amounts of blood being taken. It was a long day and seemed to take more out of me than usual. I was glad when it ended and hoped no more blood would be needed from the children.

Everything was getting so hectic. Some days I could have used an answering service, as calls were constantly coming. I usually managed to keep a level head and do what had to be done. There was no longer any such thing as a routine at our house. Wash got done late at night, when no one had anything left in their closets. Clutter collected in places that usually were neat. Ironing was done only in emergency situations. Most of the days were spent in Boston or interrupted by reporters and phone calls. One particular evening we had a visit scheduled from a cable TV channel wanting some footage on Jason. They were due at six, which meant the children would have to be fed early. Just as I was getting their meal ready a call came from a Catholic priest who wished to tell me about the powers of this "sister" he knew. He was genuinely concerned, no doubt, and I was trying to be kind, explaining my beliefs while at the same time being pressured by the relentless ticking of the clock. Needless to say, when the television crew came down the driveway, we were not ready.

The children were still eating and Wes was just getting home, full of questions as to why there was such disorganization. Eventually we were "ready" and as we came out on the front lawn the cameras began to roll. But while Wes and I were talking to the anchorman I could hear Bryan and MaryEllen crying in the house. All this confusion was not the children's fault, yet they were suffering for it. I felt like I was ready to explode!

"I'm sorry, but I just can't do this," I blurted, and dashed inside.

Wes was taken aback to say the least, but, after the crew had left and he'd heard about the way things had gone he was a little more understanding. It had not been a good day! Surprisingly enough, we heard later that the taping was a success. We never did get to see it and, in a way, I was glad.

On the 12th of August we got the results of the HLA typing for Jason's donor. Success! We were elated — and my instinctive feelings had been right! Little MaryEllen would be the one to try to save her big brother's life. She was a perfect match, and neither of the others were even close. Jason had been worried about not finding a match, and this set his mind at ease.

"I have my donor! I'm perfectly fine now!" Jason informed a reporter. "I'm glad my sister's going to give me the bone marrow. Now I know somebody will be able to help me and I don't have to worry anymore. She'll be asleep when they take it from her so she probably won't even feel it and that's good."

In the midst of all this excitement, we were anticipating seeing Walt Disney World. Jason had been granted a special wish by the High Hopes Wish Foundation, a wonderful organization dedicated to fulfilling the wishes of terminally ill children. We left on August 16th, after a bit of uncertainty as to whether we'd be leaving at all! Our flight was at 10:55 A.M. and we'd had to be at Mass General at 8:00 that morning for Jason to have a two-hour blood transfusion.

We raced through the Callahan Tunnel to Logan Airport with only minutes to spare, relieved to discover when we arrived that the flight was delayed. This gave us time to catch our breath before boarding. Finally, after a relaxing, enjoyable flight, we reached the condo that had been provided for us. It was lovely and we were glad to be there. Being so far from home without Wes was strange, but business responsibilities had made the trip impossible for him. Mom Vitale came instead, and was a tremendous help, as usual.

The children enjoyed the Magic Kingdom even in the merciless temperature. Jason, on prednisone, was very grouchy, but I think he enjoyed himself anyway. Watching him race along the mini Grand Prix raceway with his grandmother, I couldn't help but think that the next time our family visited Florida Jason might be in heaven. These thoughts were not predominant, yet every so often, when least expected, they would crowd in. This was reality. To push them aside would be to close my eyes to what was a distinct possibility. I knew God was able and I wanted to trust Him no matter what happened! As we prepared to leave Epcot Center for the airport we were caught in a torrential downpour. We were soaked. The children laughed until they could laugh no more. To them, seeing Mommy and Grammy looking like drowned rats was much funnier than the Country Bear Jamboree!

When we arrived home, Jason and MaryEllen were called in for more tests. Their white cells were fighting. Perhaps this wasn't going to work after all! It was like being on a see-saw. Up, down, up, down, up, up. It turned out to be just a fluke. Their match was indeed a good one and MaryEllen was still the donor. We heard from Washington again and were told that as far as New Hampshire's paying was concerned things looked pretty bleak. Still, they insisted there was nothing to worry about; something would open up. Publicity continued and the pace of our schedule picked up even more. We were in a race with this disease. What if there were another relapse before we found a hospital? No, God would work it out. We felt confident about that.

With such a pace it was difficult to accomplish everything. Simple things like showers had to be squeezed in. One Monday morning I had to get in the shower and get my hair washed. The children were downstairs. I checked on them and told Jason and Bethany to stay in the basement where they were playing. Bryan was entertaining MaryEllen as she sat in the walker in the living room. They would be fine for the few minutes while I was in the shower.

In the middle of my shampoo I heard an awful crash. I jumped out, grabbed a towel and ran. MaryEllen was still in the walker — at the bottom of the cellar stairs. Blood poured from her mouth. Looking down I found one of her teeth on the floor. Running upstairs with her in my arms and my towel in her mouth, I dialed the dentist. As I was talking quite hysterically I noticed the three holes that had once held her three teeth. She had lost them all! I was put in touch with an oral surgeon and made an appointment. Next I dialed Faith, for no particular reason other than panic.

She asked, "What's so funny?"

I said, "I'm not laughing, I'm crying!" Poor Faith. She pictured my finding Jason in bed not breathing. I explained what had happened and she came right over.

While we waited for her, Bryan hugged my leg and said, "Don't worry Mommy, we can get a new one with teeth."

I didn't want a new one, I wanted to go back in time and decide against the shower. The visit with the oral surgeon showed her gums were clean but the teeth could not be replaced. He tried to console us with the prediction that, by the time she was six, we would never know anything had happened, but this was small comfort. I still felt terrible. Poor MaryEllen!

With MaryEllen scheduled to be the donor, the need to find a hospital for the operation to take place became even more urgent. Publicity increased with the state's inability to help and it seemed as if the whole area was in an uproar. Perhaps it was the irate citizens that spurred the New Hampshire state government into action. This sick child was bad P.R.!

One evening we were visited by Susan Lombard, a woman

from the Office of Human Services. She was a very sweet person who was genuinely interested in helping our Jason. When she understood the whole story she promised to assist in some way, somehow. Back in her office she started a search for a hospital that would have a sympathetic view of this complicated mess.

Meanwhile, others had been touched by Jason's plight. Donations and fund-raising continued as the fund reached $50,000.00. This was wonderful, yet it still fell far short of what was required.

Then, one morning after breakfast, the phone rang. The caller asked if I were Martha Vitale and if I had a son, Jason, who needed an operation. He went on to say that he was prepared to pay for the transplant. He knew about the cost and said he would do whatever it took to see that Jason had a chance to live a normal life. The blessings he had been blessed with were many, he said. There was no need to retire and take it easy at his age so he wanted to use what he had to help those who were less fortunate than he. The memory of an eight-year-old daughter who had died from cancer had not disappeared from his mind. Why shouldn't he try to help spare another family such a loss? I was in shock as I took his name and phone number. He asked that Wes reach him later on. After all our frustration with governmental red tape, this certainly gave us a glimmer of hope once again. Was this God's answer for our crisis?

Later in the week we met this dear man, his wife and two of their sons. They were the kind of people that made us feel at ease, as though they had always been our friends. In the long months that lay ahead, the sincerity of this offer would be demonstrated time and again. Very soon after their visit we received another call from Susan. She had located a hospital in California that was most interested in Jason's case. It was the City of Hope National Medical Center, located in Duarte, California. Its approach to catastrophic illness is unique. The medical staff there believes there is no benefit to healing the body if in so doing the soul is destroyed. Money is not an object. If an operation cannot be afforded it is performed anyway.

They wanted us to contact them, and we wasted no time in doing that. Yes, they would do Jason's bone marrow transplant! With close communication between the physicians there and Dr. Truman here in Boston, Jason's condition was monitored and a date in October was discussed. It was so difficult to be patient. Time was passing, with a relapse threatening every day.

While we were waiting for a definite date, Jason returned to school. He seemed to enjoy being in the first grade. His teacher was a mother of seven, and a lovely, understanding woman. When Jason grew tired, she let him rest. When he was cross, she understood. It was a blessing that he had school to go to, as it made the time pass quickly and offered a much needed diversion from anxiety about the upcoming operation.

"I try to be brave but sometimes I can't," Jason said. "It's getting closer and closer and the worry pushes up to my head and messes it up."

In mid-September we learned definitely that Jason's operation was scheduled. We had to be in California by October 22nd for an October 23rd admission. Now it was time to start packing and to tie up loose ends in N. H. We found a friend to live in the house while we were gone. The schools were told that Jason and Bethany would be leaving. Last minute physicals were scheduled and all other matters attended to. Three to five months would be a long time away from home, yet we had been waiting for this for four months and were anxious to get moving.

We were put in touch with The Corporate Angels, a group of private planes that will transport cancer victims and their families if they are going where the patient and his family needs to go. The timing was perfect and we were connected with a very kind pilot who was more than happy to take us to California on October 19th. What more could we ask for? Hadn't God worked everything out perfectly in His own time? We could only marvel at His goodness to us and pray again for divine guidance.

CHAPTER SIX

CALIFORNIA

The packing was done, the house taken care of, the good-byes said. Watching the ground disappear below, I had a tremendous sense that life would never be quite the same again. But isn't life like that for everyone? It comes with no guarantees of smooth roads and gentle breezes. We just don't anticipate the ruts and the winds.

I looked over at MaryEllen. She was falling asleep in her car seat, which we had strapped into one of the six seats in this small jet. She seemed so little to be going so far away from those at home we all loved. She'd probably be running around by the time we returned. Now, at eleven months, she was quite mobile but didn't walk. Wes was in front of me with the other children. Bryan watched out the windows, full of wonder as the cotton-like clouds sailed by. Almost three, he seemed small to be facing this strange life ahead. Bethany, a grown-up five, tried to busy herself with sticker books and the big bag of surprises she had been given when we left home. The going away party in kindergarten had been fun but now it was all behind her and she wondered if her friends would forget her.

Then there was Jason, sitting somberly on Wes's lap, occasionally letting a few tears fall. It's hard to be brave all the time, especially when you're six years old and you don't know what's ahead.

"I'm scared, Dad. I just don't know what this is going to be like. I'm afraid it's going to be real hard for me. I don't know if I'll ever be going home again."

Wes rubbed Jason's head and spoke softly, "Jason, there are a lot of things we don't know. Shouldn't we be thankful that we have a God that knows everything? He will help us through this and He wants you to trust Him no matter how hard it gets. You have always done that and this time won't be any different as far as that goes. It's all right to feel scared. We all do. But we have Someone to turn to when we're afraid. You know who that is, don't you?"

Jason nodded. "A lot of people don't have a Savior to help them." Jason brightened and it wasn't long before he too was totally involved in the flight.

He was delighted when the pilots invited him to sit with them for a while, but when they actually let him steer the plane, that was too good to be true. He was still smiling when we landed at a little airport in Salina, Kansas, to refuel. Everything was so flat! Miles and miles of field stretched out in every direction. New England was not like that at all! A very pleasant lady in the building at the airport fed the children homemade chocolate chip cookies and let them talk to her parrot, and then we were on our way again. The scenery was breathtaking — immense patchwork quilts of fields waiting to be planted, peaks of mountains piercing the clouds, the tail of the Grand Canyon, and, finally, the many lights of Palm

Springs. California at last! Enjoyable as it had been, it was a relief to know that the flight was behind us.

Old family friends Charlie and Pat Spataro were waiting at the airport with a rented car for us. We piled all the luggage into the big station wagon and went to their house for a snack. We felt at home within minutes. The strangeness of an unfamiliar city was lost in the closeness we felt with these friends who were giving so much of themselves. Once again we were grateful for the luxury of having Christian friends. Although we would have loved to stay longer we were due in Monrovia, one hundred and twenty miles further, by nine or ten that evening. So we were off again.

"Wes, what's that ticking?"

"Oh, probably an engine noise, don't worry about it."

But when the engine noise developed into a steady banging the "don't worry about it" turned to "get off the road as fast as you can, something is really the matter with this thing!" And Wes took over the wheel. We were in San Bernadino and pulled into the first motel we saw. As we coasted into a parking space the car shuddered, coughed and died. Monrovia would not see us that night! To make matters worse, the kids had been awakened by the commotion. MaryEllen was wailing and I was soaked — one of the more dramatic lurches the car had treated us to before dying had showered me with a full cup of coffee. We settled into the motel room and started making phone calls.

Charlie felt terrible when he heard the story. "I'll take care of everything in the morning. Pat and I will bring you a new car by the afternoon."

I don't know what we would have done without him. Looking back now I'm glad the car broke down. We all had time to stop and catch our breath. We walked to a restaurant for breakfast. The children enjoyed seeing many birds and plants — especially cacti — that they had never seen before. They were sure that walking was more fun than watching everything go by through car windows.

When we finally were on our way again none of us were disappointed to be a day behind. We watched the California landscape and read the signs with interest. Every mile was leading us closer. We were anxious to begin.

Before long we pulled up in front of 818 Valley View, the house we would call home for the next several months. A modest stucco ranch, it had a beautiful lawn and gardens boasting gardenias, lilies, petunias and roses of every color. Everyone liked it immediately. Bethany noticed the swing set in the back yard and was thrilled. The boys couldn't believe that there were real oranges on the trees. It was awesome! Little MaryEllen was glad to be out of the car. She would explore everything later! We were greeted warmly by Lilyane and her parents Lily and "Monte." Lilyane had agreed to move in temporarily with her folks and let us rent her house. Once more we had Christian friends to thank for coming to our assistance.

That night, as we closed tired eyes, we were truly thankful to the God who had taken us across the entire country with four little ones, found us a place to live, a car to drive and above all a hospital that would take Jason. A few months before we had not been certain that any of this would happen. A few years before we could not have imagined that any of this would be necessary! But the Lord had known it all and had gently led us each step of the way.

CHAPTER **SEVEN**

CITY OF HOPE

It was October 22nd when we drove onto the grounds of the City of Hope National Medical Center. We were pleasantly surprised to find the atmosphere so restful. The long driveway was lined with palms and a huge expanse of flawlessly manicured lawn stretched out beyond. There were rose gardens and waterfalls on the right and a large parking lot on the left. The children thought the little tram that ran between the parking lot and the hospital was wonderful — "just like Disneyland."

In front of the main building was a big fountain with a statue of a father, mother and baby. Just to the left was a large building under construction. To the right was the pediatric building and behind all this, reaching back almost 90 acres, were areas for research. We felt immediately that we would like this new place, so different from Boston, yet so receptive to us strangers.

Since opening its doors over 70 years ago, the City of Hope National Medical Center has never turned away anyone for financial reasons. Although insurance companies are billed for the services provided by the Medical Center, individuals who cannot pay are not billed. Many fund-raisers as well as private donations support this great institution. Over 300 bone marrow transplants had been performed inside its walls and the rate of success was close to 50%. Almost all the patients were cancer victims or suffered from some other equally catastrophic illness.

The first day was for preliminary tests. The following day would be admission day and there were things that could be done in advance to make that easier. Jason and MaryEllen were the only ones that were needed but with no baby sitter we decided we would all go. Jason had an EKG, CAT scan, chest x-ray, spinal tap and bone marrow aspiration as well as the usual blood work. While these tests were not fun, he was having no problem at all compared to his dear little sister.

The trouble began with the blood work. The nurses had been told to get at least 20 cc's from her. After three or four attempts they were still getting nowhere. Her little vein would yield 4 or 5 cc's then shut down. Of course this had her screaming and fighting. She did not like these ladies who kept smiling at her and then stabbing her with needles. Finally, after the chief blood technician had been called in, it was decided to try entering her jugular vein. They wrapped her tightly, as though in a cocoon, and, suggesting that I leave the room, they tipped her upside down. As I closed the door I shut my eyes but my ears would not close. She screamed until she lost her breath. Then, as quick as a wink, it was over.

We proceeded to the EKG department. My poor baby, with a bandage on her neck, was falling asleep and woke just enough to fidget while the bands were put on her arms and legs. The EKG went fairly well except for the fact that she was still sighing heavily from crying and the lines kept jumping around. By the time her tests were completed I was feeling worn out.

We still had a meeting with the pediatrician who would be treating Jason and with the doctors who headed the Bone Marrow Transplant (BMT) unit. Dr. Foreman gave us a tour of the BMT floor and showed us the room that was soon to be Jason's. As we walked along he talked about the patients. There were no other children in the ward now but earlier we had met a little boy who was due in at the end of the month. We discussed the severity of the procedure and the fact that less than half of these rooms would be the stepping stone to health. Looking into the faces of these folks made that difficult to accept. Half of them would never leave. In which half would our Jason fit?

Dr. Foreman told us, "Any odds are 100% better than none. Why can't Jason be that one-in-ten success story?"

While the children watched cartoons in the waiting area, we met with Dr. Krance in the adjoining physician's lounge. He was nice in his own way but vastly different from our beloved Dr. Truman. His face showed little expression until he smiled. Then he was actually handsome. His thick mustache almost covered his mouth; maybe that made it hard to see his expression. We would soon become accustomed to his mannerisms. It was easy to tell that he knew what he was talking about, even if he showed little emotion.

The results of the bone marrow came back and Dr. Krance reported that it did not look good. For a minute we weren't sure we were hearing right. Dr. Truman would have said, "I have bad news." We stopped him, wanting to be sure we understood him.

"Do you mean there are leukemic cells present?"

"Yes, Jason is not disease-free but the relapse is just beginning so it could be worse."

Our immediate concern was whether or not the transplant was still on. The thought of our having traveled all that way for nothing left me weak! We had been told that a remission was needed so I was quick to assume the worst. Dr. Krance explained, however, that the transplant would be done as planned. The only change was the chance of success. It had dropped from a possible 48% to approximately 30%. He felt sure that Jason would go through the procedure with flying colors. The trouble would be the risk of relapse because of the diseased cells still in the marrow. If all these blasts were not destroyed by the radiation and chemotherapy, they would begin multiplying and the leukemia would return, even with new bone marrow.

It had been a very tiring day. We wondered what other surprises would greet us in the morning. For now, it was nice to go home and relax a little. We decided not to tell Jason about this relapse. He had enough to contend with. After all, the relapse hadn't changed anything that much. During the evening, Mom and Dad Vitale called. They were anxious to hear how we had made out. Flights had been arranged for them for the following Thursday. As they listened to the events of the day, they decided they were needed right then, not a week later. They were able to change their reservations to Thursday the 24th instead.

On Wednesday, October 23, 1985, Jason was admitted to The City of Hope. To us, it had become just what its name declares. Apart from this facility there might have been no hope. The plate on the door read Room 3218. It looked no different from rooms in a thousand hospitals throughout the country. Yet it was unique, for it was our Jason who was to stay here from now on.

For a while at least, there would be one less to tuck in at night and one less around the breakfast table. We were glad that Jason liked the room. There was plenty of space for his trucks, cars and numerous other toys. Curious George, Bumblelion and Pound Puppy had a shelf all to themselves. Jason even had his own bathroom, which was pretty special to a six-year-old.

There wasn't much for him to do that day. After a trip to the radiation department for some measurements, he was free to go out with us until bedtime. The next day was much the same except that, when we went to the airport in the evening to pick up Mom and Dad Vitale, Jason was able to come with us. What a surprise for Grammy and Grampy! They arrived at a perfect time.

On Friday, Jason went into the operating room to have a Hickman Line inserted. We usually called this a catheter, as that was basically what it was. By placing a tube into a vein in the chest and leaving one end protruding from a small hole, the need for intravenous needles was eliminated. Jason sailed through this and, other than being a bit sore, felt fine.

CHAPTER **EIGHT**

SINGING

The following Tuesday Jason began radiation treatment. He had never experienced this before. It was very interesting to watch the huge, multi-million dollar machine being set up. Being prepared for this machine made Jason look like he was dressing for Halloween. His lungs were traced in black for the placement of lead blocks. This area would not need as powerful a dose and had to be protected.

Dressed only in underpants, he stood on Styrofoam blocks and was held by straps secured to the ceiling. There were pegs for his hands to grasp, as movement was not allowed. For the first treatment special capsules that would measure the radiation were taped here and there all over him. He resembled an Indian in war paint. Radiation did not hurt. There were no apparent side effects after his first few treatments. Later the vomiting started and his appetite, which had begun to wane, disappeared completely.

Wes and I usually took turns accompanying him, as his treatments were three times a day. On Thursday evening it was my turn. My spirits were drooping and I was beginning to wonder what we were doing there. Jason, however, was in excellent spirits. As we walked to radiation he was telling jokes to the wheelchair attendant.

During the treatment, as I watched him on the monitor, I could see his lips moving. The nurses that were with me in the station outside the radiation room turned up the volume. Above the whir of the machines I heard his little voice singing. I tried to place the song but couldn't. It was an original Jason song that he made up as he went along. The only lines I could make out were "Jesus is my Savior" and "God is my Friend." As my tired eyes welled up with tears my spirits were lifted high. It was not I who was having TBI (total body irradiation) yet I was feeling down in the dumps. This desperately ill little guy had once again taught me the value of trusting in the Lord.

Friday marked the end of radiation. By then Jason was itching from dry skin and found it increasingly difficult to stand still. He was very relieved when the last radiation session was over. Saturday was chemotherapy day. While 1500 cc's of VP16 were pumped through his catheter, Jason slept. The hydrocortisone and benadryl given to avoid an allergic reaction had also made him very sleepy. The only time he woke up was to urinate. This was a task in itself due to the cardiac monitor the nurse was watching. Because he could not get to the bathroom he was forced to use the "bottle." Mr. Modest had to make sure we all left the room for this. It was quite comical to see him so concerned about his privacy at a time like that.

With twice the lethal dosage of chemotherapy going through his veins, Jason was ready for the new marrow — almost. On Sunday he was given a pass to go out for dinner with us all.

Barbie Walsh had arrived in California to write about the upcoming operation and she came along. Dinner was not that great. Jason was on a special, low bacteria diet and could not eat the things he wanted. He was glad to go back to the hospital that night.

Although Jason was thousands of miles away from home, the folks in New England were still helping. Literally hundreds of cards had arrived during the week of radiation. Surrounding him on all sides of his room were banners from classrooms in Massachusetts and New Hampshire, as well as letters and cards in all shapes and sizes. The nurses couldn't believe how popular he was. They had never seen a patient receive so much mail.

As time went by and the steady flow of mail did not abate, more hospital personnel became curious. "Who is this kid getting all this mail?"

One day the lady from the mail room paid Jason a visit. She had to find out why this little boy needed a whole box to himself when usually one would do for an entire floor. There is no proper way to express the gratitude we felt towards all those who kept Jason so very busy opening mail. We all loved the letters that children wrote from schools. Many times we laughed until we cried. When days were otherwise rather long and sad it was wonderful to have the daily mail to look forward to.

Through reporters, Jason sent a message back to the thousands of people who were praying for his recovery. "It's up to them to trust in God. Even if I die they should believe in Him all the while."

On Monday morning, November 4th, MaryEllen was admitted to The City of Hope. She was in the pediatrics building rather than where Jason was. At 7:30 A.M. on Tuesday she was taken to the operating room. While we waited in the corridor just outside the O.R. we played with her and held her. Mom Vitale had come in to see her before she went in to surgery. When the time came for her to be wheeled away she hardly whimpered. It was a very strange feeling, walking away and leaving our baby there. I would be glad when 10:00 came and she was all finished. Thinking about her being placed under anesthesia while needles extracted precious bone marrow from her tiny hips gave me chills. She was so little! Yet, when it was over, she was fine. At first she cried and thrashed around. She was so hungry that she became angry. Since she had not eaten since the night before — her frustration was understandable. After a bottle of apple juice she fell asleep.

When she awoke she was MaryEllen again, crawling down the hall and as happy as could be. A passerby would never guess she had been in surgery. Oh, there were bandages on her hips to cover more than 30 holes, and bandages on her little feet. One foot had held the I.V. while the other accepted the blood transfusion. Wes had given blood specifically for her on the day before. It would replace the 250 cc's she lost while giving the marrow. This represented 1/3 of her total bone marrow. After being filtered to remove fat and bone particles, the marrow would be given to Jason through the catheter in his chest. It is amazing to realize that this marrow would find its way to the bones on its own. What a marvelous machine the human body is! Once inside Jason's bones it would rapidly reproduce to replace his own marrow, which had been obliterated by the radiation and chemotherapy. Another amazing fact was that Jason would then have MaryEllen's blood type. Although their match was perfect, their blood types were different. His was O positive and hers was A positive. A staggering amount of research must have gone into this procedure. When we hear the Leukemia Society discussing the great need for research we now understand what this means. We feel very privileged to have been the recipients of such a tremendous effort.

CHAPTER NINE

TRANSPLANT

November 5 was what the calendar read. It was hard to imagine that eight years had gone by since Wes and I were married. That year it was hard to tell it was our anniversary. While Wes was up in Jason's room, I was with MaryEllen in hers. This was the day everything had been pointing to for weeks, even months. By 11:30 A.M. the "cranberry cocktail" (as the nurses call it) was ready. Benadryl was given to Jason and then, as the rich, red drops entered their new home, he slept.

Dad and Wes sat silently by, as if watching magic. Their faces were hidden by masks now, for the risk of infection was growing as Jason's own marrow died. There would be nothing to fight infection before many more days went by. Even as he slept, the room for isolation was being prepared. He would be moved there later on in the day. As the last marrow ran from the bag above his bed, Jason stirred. He had seen very little of this potentially life-saving procedure. I had not seen it at all, yet it was enough for me to know that it was being done.

Later on I saw my son sitting up in bed and eating popcorn. He certainly wasn't acting very ill! That evening we gathered Curious George, Pound Puppy and all the other friends and sent them to the sterilizer. They would be back the next day in plastic bags, all ready to go into isolation with Jason. The cars and trucks, MASK vehicles and G.I. Joes would be put on a shelf to wait. All the cards came down, as did the banners and posters. In the morning the room would belong to someone else; Jason was ready to move.

With I.V. pole in tow, we took one last walk along the corridor before Jason would be leaving that floor. Although he had been there more than a week, he hadn't been able to have any contact with the other patients, who were all in various stages of bone marrow transplants. We passed the room of the Chinese boy whose father often sat reading the Bible. Was that a respirator next to his bed? That usually was a sign that things weren't going well. Then there was the older man who always smiled and waved. He had been there for four months. The next room belonged to Vicki. She had just come out of isolation and had her door closed. We passed the nurses' station and talked to the ward clerk, Annette, who loved to joke and play with Jason. Almost directly across from the end of the nurses' station was the room that Jason would call his.

As he looked into the isolation room he shivered. "I'm going to get pretty cold in there."

"Why? What do you mean?"

"Well, because of all that ice. Isn't that why they call it an isolation room?"

We laughed, and giving him a hug, assured him there would be no ice and he definitely would not freeze. We kept going down the other side of the ward. There were two more isolation rooms. In one was a man named Jay who had his transplant the week before. He waved as we passed the door. Jason noticed that all his hair was gone.

"Except for the doctors and nurses," he commented, "I'm the only one with hair on this whole floor."

There were more friends to wave to and then we were back where we had started — at the door of 3218. The nurses were getting anxious. They wanted Jason in his new room.

We opened the door which led from the hall into the anteroom. This little room would hold all the toys and cards that could not enter isolation. Already the shelves were filled with familiar things. Another door entered the large room that Jason was to occupy. It was a cheery room. The bed came out from one wall and faced a wall mural of mountains and streams. Next to the bed was a comfortable-looking recliner that sloped slightly from plenty of use. Along with lots of space for medical supplies there was a VCR to help fill the many empty hours. Seemingly, every need was supplied here, shut away from the rest of the floor. From the vents in the ceiling came the steady hum of specially filtered air being circulated. Every care had been taken to keep Jason's immunosuppressive body (non-functioning immune system) free from germs. His blood counts were steadily going down until there was almost no white count at all. It would need to reach 1000 before he could return to a regular room.

Visiting would be restricted to parents and grandparents only. Strict sterilization procedures were imposed on us. We had to wash our hands with germicidal soap, and wear a gown, mask and bonnet. Nothing could be brought in with us. The door was to be kept closed and entry had to be swift so the door would only be opened for seconds.

After we got him settled into his new room, Jason and I colored some pictures and watched a Disney film. He was getting tired and so was Mommy. Also, I was not especially fond of wandering around the hospital at night, so, a little after nine, I returned to try to get some sleep on the couch in MaryEllen's room.

During that night Wes received a phone call from Jason. "Dad, I'm in big trouble now." He started to cry.

He had diarrhea in bed and was afraid the nurses would be angry. Wes told him to call the nurse and tell her, assuring him that he would be right there, that the nurse would not be upset with him and that everything would be fine. Wes arrived to find the problem taken care of. It was after 1:00 A.M. before Wes returned to bed.

On Wednesday, MaryEllen was discharged. What a relief! It had been difficult with them both in the hospital. Everything should calm down now, or so we thought. How mistaken we were! While it was easier for us with her being home, Jason was starting to look awful. His mouth was raw with sores that ran all the way down his esophagus, making it nearly impossible to speak or even swallow. His lips were so dry that they cracked open and bled. He had a fever and in general felt terrible.

Thursday morning he asked me to help him with his shower. I had a good look at his body and my heart skipped a few beats. Was this Jason? His arms and legs were scrawny, yet his abdomen appeared bloated and swollen. His neck, ankles and private area were dark brown in comparison with the rest of him. This was from the radiation. It had also left his legs looking very blotchy in colors of red and brown. His thinning hair and his poor mouth completed the sorry picture. But that picture faded as he shivered and needed to be dried. He was just as much my son now as he was when he had been an adorable two year old, rosy-cheeked and tow-headed. I must believe that he could look healthy again.

The strong pain medicine he was on became the only thing Jason looked forward to. He lay facing the clock and would start buzzing the nurses' station when it was getting close to the four hour mark. He was growing weaker all the time and slept a lot. He knew when we were with him but did little while we were there. He tried hard to be cooperative for the doctors and nurses and to be brave, but it was just getting so difficult to cope.

Jason's body hadn't started producing platelets yet, so Wes and I began donating them. This process, called platelet pheresis, involves drawing blood from a donor's arm, removing only the platelets, and feeding the blood back into the donor's other arm. Tubes running into needles in both forearms connected us to the machine. While the blood passed through the machine, the platelets were spun out of it. Since the procedure took between three and four hours and somewhat weakened us, we'd have it done on alternate days.

It was the ninth of November. A mere four days had passed since the transplant, yet so much had happened. It seemed as if Jason were starting to fall apart. He was bleeding internally. He had developed urinary problems, evident by the blood in his urine. His temperature was 103 degrees, and he was vomiting blood. Cultures were done on blood and urine. Antibiotics were increased as was the pain medication. He only waited three hours between dosages. The I.V. pumps were kept busy with anywhere from four to nine different bottles dripping at once. He was having trouble waking up as he was sleeping so soundly from the medications. It was not uncommon for the bed to be wet because he could not wake up in time. His speech, if he spoke at all, was slurred and often made no sense. Usually he reverted to sign language because that was not so painful.

Gradually, Jason was slipping away from us. The fever often raged over 104. Blood vessels burst beneath his skin, making him look as though he had purple polka-dots. If he sneezed, the room was showered with blood and it was difficult to get his nose to stop bleeding. He knew that his hair was falling out and, rather than having it shaved, he decided to help it along by lying there and pulling it out. That was ghastly! Eventually Wes talked him into having the rest of it shaved because it was getting in his mouth and everywhere else.

Time seemed to be dragging by painfully. We wanted to see some progress or just some hopeful sign, but nothing happened. It was hard to sit idly by, unable to change anything, only waiting. The platelets were being pumped in every day, often to no advantage. My platelets were not causing his blood counts to change at all. Wes's only worked occasionally, so an anonymous man started to give platelets every other day for him. This was the most effective of all and we were so thankful that this individual was willing to go through the procedure so unselfishly. Later this man came to visit Jason and we were able to thank him, but I must admit our words seemed very inadequate.

In spite of the platelets beginning to help, Jason was feeling no better. The fight was getting harder for him. Everything hurt and was so difficult to endure. One morning as we sat waiting for him to finish in the bathroom I heard,

"Help me! Help me!"

Running to the door and throwing it open I was surprised to find him sitting there as if nothing were wrong.

"What's wrong? I thought I heard you call for help."

Looking rather annoyed, he said, "I wasn't talking to you. I was asking God to help me so this wouldn't be so hard for me."

I withered. He knew who to go to when the going got rough. What could I do to help him? He turned to the only One who could help him be strong and fight against such seemingly insurmountable odds.

He was concerned that people might forget to pray for him. He asked his Grammy on one of her visits, "Do you pray for me?"

"I most certainly do and there are hundreds of others who do, too."

"Will you pray for me right now?" When she did, with a lump in her throat, he thanked her, patting her hand and saying he felt better.

Calls came from home every day. Everyone was anxious for

some good news.

"Yes, he still had the fever. No, his blood counts were not any better, his mouth was still sore" and so it went.

By the 15th of November we were preparing ourselves for the fact that this was not going to get better. While we did leave it in God's hands, we were realistic.

Jason's little body could not keep going much longer. His body would soon go into toxic shock from having had a fever for almost a week.

Aware of his critical situation, he asked Wes, "Dad, am I going to die today?"

"I don't know, honey. Only the Lord knows that."

"I was just wondering... I know things are really bad."

The stress of all this affected us differently. Wes busied himself straightening out the room. He opened the linen closet, re-folded all the sheets and towels, tidied up the medicine cart and made Jason's bed look like Sleeping Beauty's. There wasn't a crease or a wrinkle anywhere. This behavior was anything but normal and it made me nervous. My reaction was completely the opposite. I had always had some cross-stitching or other needlework to keep me busy because I found inactivity almost unbearable. Yet on that particular November day I sat watching Jason slowly fading away and did nothing. A pleasant young nurse, Marcy, came by to visit, having been assigned to study Jason's case as part of her education. She quietly sat beside me and, noticing Wes's compulsive neatness, told me that was his way of coping. The doctors began coming in more frequently. They said the next few hours would be decisive. We would either see a complete turn around in Jason or . . .

As we left his room that night we did not know if we would see him in the morning. Our emotions were many and varied. We felt an incredible desire to see Jason well again, coupled with a very tired feeling and a longing for things to change no matter what. Suspended like this between life and death was fraying our nerves.

We prayed fervently that tomorrow would be better and fell asleep totally exhausted.

Wes woke up early and quickly dialed the hospital to see how Jason was. He could not believe what he heard. Incredibly, Jason's temperature was 93! That was eleven degrees lower than the previous day. We were thrilled. The fever was gone but he seemed much the same, just cooler. He began to hallucinate, speaking of shooting guns and finding dimes and quarters on the sheets between his legs. Even to him, it was very confusing when he would "come to" in the middle of a ridiculous conversation, not having the slightest idea what he had been talking about. In one sense it was comical; yet to think about why he was like that nearly made me cry.

Slowly Jason began to improve. His mouth healed and he could speak with less effort. His urine began to clear and he perked up a bit. Little by little he was coming back. By November 19th, the door of his room could be opened. His blood counts had risen high enough to let him out of isolation. We were surprised because we had assumed that by the time the door was opened he would be feeling much better. However, at least he was making some progress. Two days later he tried to eat something. He had not had a bite of food since he had started radiation almost a month before. French toast was the first thing he ate and the one or two bites he took could hardly be called eating. He said it tasted like cardboard and pushed it away. We had to remember that his taste buds were not functioning since they had not been used in such a long time. There wasn't much point in eating if he couldn't tell what he had in his mouth.

On November 23 Jason left isolation completely. He moved to a regular room that he referred to as "Jay's old room" because Jay had been in it before his transplant. Once he made the move he must have felt better because he decided to eat. His first meal of any substance was a bowl of "Cap'n Crunch" cereal.

I was amazed that he would choose cereal after having had

such a sore mouth. However, with only a few grimaces of pain, he finished it all.

With Jason coming along — finally — we started to prepare for Thanksgiving. Dr. Krance said if Jason felt up to it we could take him out for a few hours on the holiday. That sounded too good to be true. Actually, it turned out to be just that, for the day before Thanksgiving Jason developed a fever. On Thanksgiving day his fever was 103 and Jason spent the holiday in the hospital. Strange as it may seem, he did not mind being there. It had become home to him and offered security. The people there could take care of him better than I. As for the rest of us, we all had a normal Thanksgiving dinner. The children had a great time with Indian head bands and Pilgrim hats that Grammy made.

Later on we all went to visit Jason. The policy was that all visitors wear masks but since MaryEllen would not keep hers on we made Jason wear one too. Bethany, Bryan and MaryEllen really loved that visit with Jason. They told him about everything they could think of, smiling constantly and asking how he was and "What was this for?" and, "What does the nurse do with that?" It was a nice break for Jason as well, since it gave him something else to think about. As we left the hospital that Thanksgiving night, we were truly thankful for so many things. While the future was at best uncertain, we had seen God's hand in so many ways and felt such strength from above that we were profoundly grateful.

During the next few days we noticed changes in the condition of Toni, the patient in the room next to Jason. We had spoken with her at the brunch the nurses held before Thanksgiving. She had brought her husband and two little girls with her, although she herself was unable to eat because of all the bacterial precautions. She had talked about possibly going home right after the holiday and of feeling wonderful. But since Thanksgiving we hadn't seen her leave her room. Her husband looked somber, rather than happy. Then we saw the respirator being moved into her room and knew she was in trouble.

We learned she had pneumonia and would not be going home — ever. Within the next few days Toni slipped away from us. With her mother kneeling beside her and her husband standing helplessly by, she died. It was very sad. How do you get up and walk away from a situation like that?

I wanted to do something but could only say, "I'm so sorry." In this place where death was not uncommon, life went on as usual.

Her room was occupied again, this time by a 21- year- old boy who had had a transplant the year before. His leukemia had returned and he was planning to undergo another transplant. This was hard for us to comprehend, having seen what just one was like. We waved to him when we passed his room and then thought we saw him walking in the halls. Finally we realized that he had an identical twin. We never got to know him well for, before long, his door was closed. One night there was crying and yelling coming from the room. It sounded awful. Then I heard a nurse talking about renal failure. The next day he passed away. There would be no second chance. These sad incidents made us so thankful that we still had Jason, yet they made us realize that we should treasure each moment because there were no guarantees.

CHAPTER TEN

ANOTHER BIRTHDAY

With the fever gone, Jason was able to start going out for brief periods of time. The Sunday after Thanksgiving was a perfect day for a walk. We got him up and dressed and were surprised to find that his pants would not go around him. While he was basically thin, his stomach was terribly bloated from prednisone and other drugs he was on. We did the best we could and put his jacket on. He was not too happy about going outside. It was difficult to pull away from such sheltered conditions for the first time.

As we walked through the rose gardens he perked up. It must have felt good to do what the rest of us were doing. He noticed all the different colors in the gardens and watched a fountain spraying. After 30 minutes or so he was ready to go in. He looked exhausted. We learned just how exhausting this trip was, for he slept from 3:00 that afternoon through the night and for most of the next day.

Still, he was making progress and continued coming out on passes for rides and trips to the house. He had to wear a mask constantly at first and then was allowed to take it off at home when just the immediate family was present. Many precautions had to be taken as Jason's immune system was rebuilding itself and could not fight infection well. He could eat nothing that had been exposed to the environment, which excluded most produce and fresh foods. Everything that he used, like cereal, had to be closed tightly and used only by him. Being a rather fussy eater to begin with, Jason hated this diet. It seemed that everything he craved was off limits to him.

Gradually, we learned to cope with this and get him to eat, but it was very slow. The doctors were trying to get him ready to come home for Christmas but they warned him repeatedly that, if he wasn't eating, he couldn't leave. Other than the appetite problem, there were those fevers. Little by little, he was being weaned from antibiotics, yet every time they were stopped Jason got a fever.

There were two other boys his age on the floor. Gary, a smiley, sandy-haired little guy, was in isolation and seemed to be coming along with very little trouble in comparison to Jason. Ryan, an Oriental boy with a sweet, round face framed with dark black hair, was going through radiation and would come and visit Jason in the doorway of the room. Early one morning we walked in to find the two of them camped out in the hallway, on a sheet, playing with their trucks. Jason was wearing a mask but if I shut my eyes I would have thought I was listening to two healthy boys playing in our living room. They were having a lot of fun together. By the time Ryan was ready for isolation Jason had to move again. His bed was needed for a new BMT patient. Since he still could not go home, he went over to pediatrics. He missed the familiar nurses and liked to visit them when he could.

With Christmas just around the corner, and the thought that Jason would soon be home with them, the children were very excited. But when Christmas Eve arrived, Jason had a slight fever. The doctors agreed to let him go home for Christmas day, but he'd have to return for the night so they could check him. On Christmas morning Wes went to pick him up while the rest of the family waited, not so patiently, for them to return. Many friends and family members had sent packages and it wasn't easy for the children to just sit there gazing at them! Finally, at 10:00 they came in. Needless to say there was a lot of commotion that day! We had numerous phone calls connecting us with special people far away. While we heard reports of snow, ice and freezing temperatures in New England, we played outside in 85 degree weather. Christmas did seem strange in that environment, but I'm sure I could get used to it very easily. It had been a special day — one we hadn't been sure we would all see together.

By 6:00 P.M. Jason was begging to go back to the hospital. He complained of being tired and of stomach pain. Fortunately, once he got back there, the pain went away. After a quiet night, he was given a thorough examination. His temperature was normal, and the doctors felt that his appetite might increase faster at home. So, on December 26, 1985, Jason walked away from the hospital, free!

I had been taught to inject heparin into his catheter (to prevent clotting) and to clean the hole in his chest. Once I got used to it, it was a very simple procedure. To reduce the risk of infection, he slept in a cot in our room, away from the other children. Of course, he went back for checkups very frequently and his weight, along with many other more intricate things, was monitored. At first we had our doubts about his staying at home because he was not even trying to eat. But we forced him to drink milk shakes and eat every fattening thing we could concoct. After a few weeks our efforts paid off, and he started gaining weight.

He had perked up tremendously in the short time he had been home. He ran and played just like the others. It was wonderful! In the quiet times his little mind never stopped. One day he and I had an interesting chat on the way to a store. He began reminiscing about how the children in kindergarten had made fun of him sometimes. I reaffirmed the fact that they had not known or understood what was wrong with him.

He said, "Well, I just think it's like when Jesus said, 'Father forgive them for they know not what they do.' "

I was shocked! He had absorbed so much in his short life. Not too many 6-year-olds would consider what Jesus might say. I wondered how many adults would?

As February approached, and Jason continued to improve, we grew restless. California was wonderful, but it was not home. Jason had wanted to be home by his birthday, on the 7th, but as the days went by, that possibility looked more and more unlikely. Bethany had finished her gymnastic class at the YMCA. Bryan was growing tired of the swings, and everything was pointing eastward. Grammy and Grampy left for home, and our friends were all starting to ask when we would be leaving. Checkups were getting farther and farther apart. Finally, the first week in February, we were told we could make travel arrangements. Needless to say, we were all very excited! We scheduled a flight with The Corporate Angels, to leave L.A. on the 13th of February.

Jason was resigned to celebrating his seventh birthday on the West Coast. We had his party at the home of Debbie Perez, one of our new friends. When she learned that we hadn't tried Mexican food during our stay, she prepared a feast. We stuffed ourselves on enchiladas, tamales, guacamole, refried beans, tortillas, and countless other traditional dishes. It was a thoroughly enjoyable birthday party that ended rather unusually, with a Bible study. Debbie's friends and neighbors had been coming to her home monthly to discuss the Bible with a friend of hers, Tom Baker, who had been a missionary in El Salvador. We found their questions and interest in God's Word heart-warming, and at the end of the discussion left for home tired but refreshed.

The next day we had some very disappointing news from the Corporate Angels. The flight on the 13th had been permanently canceled, and we'd have to wait indefinitely for another date. We immediately began checking into commercial flight schedules that would fit with Jason's final checkup date, not wanting to delay our return home one day longer than we had to.

On Saturday evening we went to Tom and Nelly Baker's home in Alhambra, another suburb of L.A. Jason had a grand time with their two boys. They skate-boarded up the driveway, ran, jumped and rough-housed to their hearts' content. While the children were all playing outside, we enjoyed watching slides of El Salvador. We were intrigued with the country's primitive beauty and many cultural differences. When the evening came to an end, the children were totally exhausted, and we all took happy memories away with us.

Sunday was quite busy. I didn't give much thought to Jason's complaints of pains in his side when I considered all the activity of the night before. Was it any wonder something hurt? We took a ride to the Queen Mary in Long Beach. The children were impressed with her size and beauty. Jason seemed to enjoy the day and didn't say anything else about aches until evening. As he got ready for bed he started to cry. We could hardly touch his side without his moaning in pain. Wes took him to the hospital immediately.

Before long he called to say that Jason was very upset and wanted me. Lilyane, the woman from whom we rented the house, agreed to watch the children for me and I went over to the hospital. Jason thought he was dying because he had seen the doctors whispering together and feared the worst. They reassured him he was not dying — he had shingles. He was put in the infectious disease wing to protect the rest of the patients. An I.V. for the necessary drugs had to be started. Wouldn't you know that the Hickman line had been removed just two days earlier! Finding a good vein was no small task and actually became the worst part of this whole incident. Finally, with his ankle at a strange pitch, a vein was located and the necessary connection was made. Jason settled down, the crisis past.

Then the nurses' station called to say that we were wanted on the phone. It was Lilyane. MaryEllen had not stopped screaming since I'd left. Poor Lilyane was not used to this and was completely frazzled. I told her I would be right there and sped home to find MaryEllen still screaming! As soon as I picked her up she quieted down but sobbed for hours after she fell asleep. Perhaps she thought I had finally gone away for good. Any time I'd left her before she had her Grammy. Just after MaryEllen dozed off, Wes arrived. Lilyane must have sensed the tension we were feeling because she spontaneously asked if she could pray with us. She put her arms around the two of us and just asked the Lord to help us in this situation. It was sweet of her to want so much to do something for us.

The next week was hectic. We truly appreciated all the help Mom had been. With no one there to take her place, Wes and I became like two ships that pass in the night. When he was home, I was at the hospital, and vice-versa. He had to cook and clean up kids, etc. His life took a different course very quickly. There was no mother there to say, "I'll do it." I was impressed with the good job he did. Those pork chops he made were much better than mine. However, that rat-race pace was not for me. I felt sorry for families that had to live like that all the time. Meanwhile, Jason was almost enjoying the stay in the hospital this time. Little Gary, his friend from the BMT floor, had shingles too and was in the next room. They sent notes to each other and talked on the phone. Having someone else in the same boat sure helped the time pass quickly for both of them. After only a week, to our tremendous relief, Jason was discharged and we were free to leave California.

CHAPTER ELEVEN

HOME AGAIN

The flight home was uneventful. As the plane neared Boston our excitement rose. There are no words to explain how we felt. Life would be different now. Would we adjust to being a normal family again? Would everyone be shocked by Jason's appearance? All the anxieties quickly faded as we walked out of the tunnel that led from the plane into the building. There were banners and balloons and so many friends waiting for us.

Jason was beaming — "Is this all for me?! It seems like I've been away a year!"

We all were kissed and hugged and welcomed back in grand style. Our faithful reporter, Barbie, was there and never stopped crying until we were on the way home to New Hampshire. She had seen Jason lying alone in isolation and now here he was, laughing and jumping and thrilled to finally see the beloved faces of his New England relatives and friends.

In the house there were more banners and the following day there were more reporters. Everyone wanted to share in the excitement. Jason was filmed throwing snowballs and sledding. California hadn't been too good for that!

"I just want to get back to my normal self — do everything that I used to do — running around, swinging, playing, jumping. Hopefully, I've said goodbye to my leukemia for good!"

Normal. How does one go about returning to normalcy? For me the transition was difficult. That is not easy to admit even today. True, I was thankful to be home, but it took time to get used to being alone. I had become accustomed to having Wes around all the time and had to readjust to his going back to work. Eventually life settled down and I relaxed. Bethany returned to kindergarten and Jason was given a tutor for the rest of the school year to avoid having to repeat first grade. He enjoyed the time spent with her and seemed to be making progress. Yet when he was evaluated later on it was felt that it would be better for him to reenter first grade the following September. At first he strongly objected to this decision, but when he was told he'd be able to have Mrs. Pendergast again he decided he liked the idea.

Jason was adjusting medically as well as socially. Hospital visits were every two weeks for the first few months and then once a month. This was very different from the multiple visits he had been making every day in the weeks before we came home. Everything was checking out perfectly. The blood counts were fine and the only medications he was on were folic acid and bactrim to help avoid infections. Those were medicines anyone could have been on, far different from the powerful chemotherapy he was used to.

With each passing day we could see Jason steadily regaining his health. The puffiness in his face disappeared and his hair started growing in thick and curly. Aside from a bacterial infection that put him in the hospital for Memorial Day, Jason sailed smoothly through the next few months. September came. Bethany and Jason went off to school. As I watched them walk hand in hand to the school bus, tears came to my eyes. Last year I wasn't sure I'd ever see Jason leaving on the first day of school again. As the bus pulled away I paused to give God thanks once more for being so good to us. The happiness was overwhelming! Jason really was better! I remembered his wish for people to think he was just a regular kid. Would they?

CHAPTER TWELVE

PEACE IN THE STORM

November, 1986, marked one year since Jason's transplant. He was doing fine. School was great fun. Hospital visits were monthly and uneventful and Jason was happy. He started working with the Leukemia Society in the annual telethon and other fund-raising events. His involvement enabled us to meet many wonderful people whose lives had been touched by the disease. There were Paul and Joan, a young married couple whose niece had leukemia. Paul had raised money for the society by running across the state. Debbie and Jon had a daughter who was just finishing a transplant. They had gained courage through reading about Jason in the papers, having admired him even before their daughter was diagnosed. Tony had passed the eight-year point in remission and had become a doctor. The list went on and on. Everyone played a special role for us, whether we helped them or they helped us. It was comforting to meet others that understood.

The following letter from "Jim" in Salem, MA, was typical of the reaction people had to Jason and his circumstances:

Dear Jason,

I am writing this letter to thank you for the influence you have had on my life. Even though we never met, you have changed my outlook on life perhaps more than anyone else I am acquainted with. I have followed your plight through the many articles written in the Lawrence Eagle Tribune and I am eternally grateful. Your ability to cope and your faith in God are an inspiration to us all. I have not been, for most of my life, a religious person, but you have instilled in me a new-found faith in the Lord and His ways. I believe that through you He has reached me in a way only His wisdom could know. The unquestioning faith that you have exhibited moves me beyond what words can describe and this in someone as youthful as you is a testimony to His power.

It is difficult for me to comprehend what purpose I have in His plan but you certainly inspired in me something I could not have accomplished without your influence. I pray that He will allow me to serve in a way that will help show others what I have learned through you.

In His name,

Jim

There had been serious business problems earlier in the year which led Wes to change jobs and we felt that perhaps a total change would do us all good. On February 1st we moved to Saugus, Massachusetts. Wes was promoted in the company he was with and felt comfortable with his new responsibilities. We had prayed for guidance, as we really did want to be where the Lord wanted us. Relocating brought us closer to the Saugus Gospel Hall, and to beloved friends there. Our new home was a white house with a front porch, something I had always wanted. It was in a rural setting with woods and marsh and was perfect for us. Again, we were so thankful for the way things had turned out.

The children adjusted to their new school immediately. I still can't believe how they reacted to the move. Perhaps I had borrowed fears from my childhood. I vividly remember moving when I was in the second grade. It was anything but calm. Every morning I cried all the way to school. My children surprised me by their rapid adjustment and I thought it was wonderful.

The year passed by and before long Wes and I were coming up to our 10th anniversary. It didn't seem possible, but the year was 1987, so it had to be. Where had the time gone? Now we had been together for ten years. We also realized that the date of November 5 meant that Jason's transplant was two years behind us. That was significant. Studies had been done that showed that most patients that reach two years do not relapse. While we had always known that, statistically, Jason could — and perhaps would — relapse, we started to think that just maybe he was really cured. On November the 5th itself Jason made a public service announcement for the Leukemia Society. It was filmed in a blood donor room as Jason and a sportscaster, Mike Dowling, talked about the need for Leukemia research. His father had died from the disease when Mike was eight — Jason's age. Jason did a fine job and everyone told him he looked wonderful.

His comment was, "Sometimes people look at me and say I look wonderful, it's a miracle I look so good. They smile at me and, of course, I smile back because I'm glad too."

We spent the evening with Paul and Marie, friends and old neighbors who lived near the studio where this program had been taped. We had planned to officially celebrate our anniversary over the weekend. We spent Friday night in the same hotel we stayed in on our wedding night. Wes's mother stayed with the children. It was very nice to share a wonderful dinner and night away from the rest of the family. When we came home the following day they had made cards and written notes to us. They were so proud of themselves, as were we.

The following week was Jason's hospital visit. Bryan, Jason and I arrived at the Mass General. The boys were listening to a tape as we pulled into the parking space. We climbed out of the van I drive and closed the doors. Just as the last door slammed I became aware of an engine running.

Pointing to the car next to us, I said, "That person must have left their engine running."

As the words left me I realized the noise was coming from the van. This was by far the most ridiculous thing I had ever done. What in the world could I do? We walked into the hospital and I thought I would first call Wes, who was traveling to Springfield. Fortunately, Wes has a car phone, and I was able to reach him on the Mass Pike. He did not take too kindly to the news nor to the idea of bringing me his keys, and suggested I try to find help and call him back before he went out of range. But help was not to be found. No one could break into an Astro van with stationary side windows, so I called Wes back. I took Jason upstairs to the doctor's office, explained the crazy situation, and left him. They would do his blood tests and exam while I waited with the van. Half an hour later Wes drove up with the spare keys, shaking his head at his scatter-brained wife. Later on we'd be thanking God in amazement that my absentmindedness was His way of making sure Wes would be with me for the consultation with the doctor.

After Jason was examined I showed the nurses his recent newspaper article celebrating his second anniversary. Their reaction was a bit odd. They did not seem as happy as I had expected and they did not look me in the eye. We went in to see Dr. Kretschmar, who had only recently taken over Jason's case while Dr. Truman was away for a year. We read concern on her face. She explained that during the exam they noticed that one testicle was larger than the other. She wanted a surgeon to look at it and possibly get a biopsy.

We asked what the problem might be.

Again we heard the dreaded words, "It might be leukemia."

As we waited for Dr. Lee, the surgeon, my mind raced back over the last few years. Had we come so far only to find out we were no better off than we were four years ago? I could not imagine repeating those years a second time and I prayed that the surgeon would give us encouraging news. We all liked Dr. Lee right away. He began laughing and joking with Jason and Bryan as soon as he met them. After examining Jason carefully he decided that the smaller of the testicles might be abnormally small due to the past treatments. Just to be sure, he would do a biopsy. The appointment was made for the following week. We left his office and returned to the clinic.

As we neared the office we met Sue.

After Wes and the boys had walked past, she turned to me. "Mrs. Vitale, do you believe this — I am so tired of this! We go along so well for so long and then. . . . . " Her voice trailed off.

Why shouldn't she be tired of this? Working so hard to fight cancers, trying to keep these children alive only to fall back so many times had to be terribly discouraging. I told her what Dr. Lee said. Sue was hopeful but cautious. She had been in this field long enough to know the danger signs. I sensed that she leaned towards the theory that something was wrong. Jason's bone marrow was clean. The slides had been read from the aspiration that morning and there was no leukemia. His spinal fluid was also clear and his blood counts were good. All we needed was that biopsy.

Once more our family and friends reached out to help us. Everyone wanted to do something to keep us from feeling let down and alone. It was reassuring to know that we had so many caring people around us. We told Jason what was happening, that it might be nothing but that it could also mean a relapse. We explained about the biopsy as well. None of the news seemed to bother him. He wanted to get the biopsy over with but was not worrying.

"God will do what is best," he said and left it at that.

When we returned for the surgery, Jason, all smiles, talking about riding four wheelers, went off with the doctor. An hour later he was back, a very different little boy. The anesthesia made him feel generally miserable. It was so hard to wake up. He was sore and whiney and thirsty. Somehow we managed to dress him and take him home. The pathology would not be completed until the next day. So, again we waited, but not so patiently.

Finally, the following afternoon, we got the results. Actually Wes had called the doctor from a business appointment and was on his way home to tell me when I, having heard nothing from the doctor, called them as well. Dr. Kretschmar apologized for not having called me. Having spoken with Wes, she had assumed he would tell me.

"Basically, the biopsy showed that there is leukemia there."

Leukemia there . . . leukemia there . . . . The words pounded in my head as I very calmly asked what we were to do now. No real answers came.

"We'll have to wait and find out more about this. Not many transplant patients have had testicular relapses and there is very little data. Tomorrow we'll be contacting other doctors in transplant centers."

Leukemia there . . . leukemia there . . . .

Wes drove in the driveway. His mother was there, outside with the children. When she came in we told her. She seemed to shrivel. Wes told her all that we knew. He said we didn't know what was ahead and that God would give all of us strength. With the Lord's help, we had done it before and could do it again. Wes's words pounded in my head as well, "do it again . . . do it again . . ."

I wanted to yell, "Be quiet, just stop talking!!!"

But instead I nodded. I did not want to do it again and, for the first time in our experience, I did not want Jason to be sick again. Why were we going around in circles? Why had we been given these two years if he was to be taken anyway? My strength was gone now. I, who always tried to be prepared for things like relapses, had actually been caught off guard.

When we left California we had known what the chances of relapse were. Jason had a 25% chance to live beyond five years. That left a 75% chance for relapse. I had accepted that and almost expected it. However, as time went on, it grew easier to believe otherwise. When two years had passed I started to think that Jason had indeed won the battle. The timing of this relapse was terrible. I did not know how to deal with my emotions. Perhaps exhaustion played a great part in how I felt. Just thinking about the past and imagining the future left me feeling like I was too tired to go on. If only the world could stop and give me time out. Everything was happening so quickly that it was becoming a blur.

There were no answers this time. Always before we had known what we were aiming for. What now? How could we explain this to a nine-year-old when it made no sense to us? Wes called Jason downstairs and the three of us went into the living room. Jason rested on the couch as we sat very close by. Wes told him that we had heard from the doctors and that there was leukemia there.

He looked up at his dad, wrinkling up his cheeks, "There is?"

Wes nodded and went on to say that we weren't sure what was going to happen and that we needed to trust God more than ever. Jason acted like that was the only natural thing to do.

He asked about chemotherapy. We told him that the doctor thought that would be the treatment or at least part of it. Jason thought about that for a minute. A few tears ran silently down his cheeks.

He wiped them away and quietly said, "I don't want to do that again."

How could we blame him? I had never had chemotherapy or spinal taps or bone marrows and I didn't want to go through this

105

again, either. This poor little boy had been through so much yet he was not breaking down, just simply voicing what we all felt. Unfortunately, we all agreed that we didn't have a choice. We also agreed to do what the doctors said because they had much more experience with diseases like leukemia than we did. Jason resolved to be brave and trust God no matter what. We would have to do the same.

It was a frustrating time for everyone involved. We were used to having an established plan of attack, not indecision and confusion over treatment. Jason was scheduled for two weeks of daily radiation treatments, to be followed by a three year chemotherapy protocol. But, on our first appointment with the radiation department, I suspected something was wrong. They examined Jason, asked a lot of questions and told us to go home and come back tomorrow. There were some things they needed to discuss with Jason's doctor.

Before the appointment on the following day we received a call from Dr. Kretschmar. She explained that the radiation department was very uneasy about giving Jason radiation. The doctors in California had been contacted and it was the general opinion that the amount of radiation needed to kill the leukemia in the testes, added to the amount previously given, would cause very unpleasant, chronic side effects. These could include rectal fissures, diarrhea, etc. It sounded awful. So radiation had to be ruled out. That left surgery and chemotherapy. The best thing to do would be to remove both testicles, thus removing the leukemia. Following that up with a protocol that included many drugs Jason had already had, it was felt that he would have a 10% chance of surviving. While that wasn't much, it was much better than nothing. We did not have a choice. We felt a sadness in the surgery, though, because it was taking away part of his body. I couldn't help but feel a bit guilty as he was wheeled away once more to the operating room.

A few nights after Jason's surgery, I sat in our weekly prayer meeting at the Gospel Hall, feeling exhausted and defeated. Just when everything seemed to be going so well, disaster struck. Why was life so unfair?

Shortly before the meeting closed a passage of scripture was read: *"And the same day, when the even was come, He saith unto them, 'Let us pass over unto the other side.' And when they had sent away the multitude, they took Him even as He was in the ship... And there arose a great storm of wind, and the waves beat into the ship, so that it was now full. And He was in the hinder part of the ship, asleep on a pillow; and they awake Him and say unto Him, 'Master, carest thou not that we perish?' And He arose and rebuked the wind, and said unto the sea, 'Peace be still.' And the wind ceased, and there was a great calm. And he said unto them, 'Why are ye so fearful? How is it that ye have no faith?' And they feared exceedingly, and said one to another, 'What manner of man is this that even the wind and the sea obey him?'"* (Mark 4:35-41)

The Lord used these verses to speak to my weary heart. Surely He knew all about the storm when He said *"Let us pass over unto the other side."* The disciples should have realized that and trusted Him. He certainly did not intend for them to perish. Perhaps they missed out on something by being so afraid. Suddenly it all fit together. The Lord understood! He knew about every storm in this passing over and He was there. He wanted me to trust Him, for He was in control. He alone was able to stop the winds and calm my fears. I realized, with shame, He could say to me precisely what He said to those men that day, *"Why are ye so fearful? How is it that you have no faith?"* No one knew what a change had taken place in my outlook that night. I was ready to face tomorrow because the Lord of Heaven cared for me and for my little son.

God seemed to be preparing Jason as well for the coming storms. One day he approached Wes in the upstairs hallway at home. He had just been reading his Bible and said, smiling, "You know, Dad, you have never disappointed me, but you could. God has never disappointed me, and he can't."

Not long after the surgery the chemotherapy began. Fortunately a port-a-cath had been inserted in Jason's chest while he was in the operating room. This device enabled intravenous drugs to be given without searching for a vein, making life easier for Jason. The drugs in the new protocol were not difficult to tolerate. The one exception was ARA-C.

This drug was infused subcutaniously for four days in his abdomen. Jason had to wear a small pump around his waist during that entire period. The dreaded procedure was repeated every eight weeks. The side effects of the treatment, low blood counts and infection, caused him to be hospitalized more than once. Eventually the drug was eliminated, which was a cause for celebration.

CHAPTER THIRTEEN

REBECCA

Time passed, and once more we fell into the routine of juggling life around hospital visits. It wasn't easy, as we were expecting a new baby in the spring and I was extremely tired all the time. Jason looked forward to the new baby. At ten he really would fill the big brother role well. He, as well as the rest of us, was interested to see how the "tie count" of boys and girls in the family would be broken.

As May approached, we filled the nursery with baby things and waited. It had been a long time since we had a baby in the house and the excitement grew. While everything seemed fine, medically, I experienced a sense of uneasiness that I can't explain.

Monday evening, May 8th, my labor started while Jason and Wes were out for a walk. I rested, waiting for them to come home.

When they returned we telephoned Jacki Smith to come stay with the children. She arrived quickly and we were off to the hospital. Other than shaking with chills, I was feeling quite well. It was nearing 1 A.M. by the time I was settled in the birthing room. As I undressed I prayed for safety, realizing how much the children needed me.

The doctor came in and tried to get the fetal monitor working. He asked the nurse to check it. Something was wrong. He was suddenly nervous and demanding. The electrode he had inserted to find the baby's heartbeat was not working either. Beep… Beep… Beep… it sounded. An alarm was going off inside my head as well! This baby was dead! The doctor did not say that but rather yelled for an I.V. nurse and began to wheel me out of the room, explaining as he went.

"No time for a spinal, Martha, we must get that baby out now! You will have a C section under general anesthesia."

I nodded in agreement, knowing that I did not have a choice. The urgency in his voice said so much. He was a soft spoken gentleman who was now giving orders like a sergeant.

The anesthesiologist arrived and, with very little explanation, told me to breathe into the mask and count backwards from one hundred. One hundred..ninety nine..ninety eight..a coldness in my arm...ninety seven.

"Martha, Martha can you wake up, Martha?" Someone was calling me, but who? Oh yes, I was in the hospital. I opened my eyes to see Wes leaning over me.

I asked, "She's dead, isn't she?"

Wes shook his head. "No, she's alive, but she's very sick."

I can't recall being told we had a baby girl. Perhaps another conversation had taken place as I fought to come out of the fog I was in. Little Rebecca Naomi was indeed very sick. She had been without a heartbeat for thirteen minutes. A special team from Boston Children's Hospital came to take her to their neonatal nursery.

Minutes before they left, they brought her to my room. As long as I live I will never forget looking down into her darling little face and holding her velvet hand. She was so beautiful.

As I took her hand and whispered, "You poor little thing," I ached to hold her. Never had I wanted anything as much as I wanted her to live.

Initially we were told that Rebecca might wake up all of a sudden and eventually be fine. However, as the hours turned to days, she grew worse. The tests showed no brain activity and she was having seizures repeatedly. Though I was still hospitalized and in a great deal of pain due to the infection I had, Wes agreed to take me to see her at Children's Hospital. As we sat holding her we wished that time would stop. How it hurt to give her back to the nurse. We realized that nothing could be done for Rebecca. It had been decided that her life support systems would be shut off on the following day.

When we returned to Children's Hospital the calendar read Friday, May 12. Four days earlier Rebecca wiggled and kicked waiting to be born. Now she lay waiting to die. There are no accurate words to describe the hurt I felt as her mother. It was so comforting to have our mothers and my sister Becky and her husband Dale with us that morning. They were able to see our baby and to love her for a little while. We all moved to a conference room and waited for the team of nurses and doctors to bring Rebecca.

As we waited Wes took a Bible from the shelf and read Psalm 27: *"The Lord is my light and my salvation; whom shall I fear? The Lord is the strength of my life; of whom shall I be afraid?... I had fainted unless I had believed to see the goodness of the Lord...be of good courage and He shall strengthen thine heart; wait I say on the Lord."*

The words of the Psalm soothed me. I gained a greater appreciation for my husband that day. He too was broken-hearted, yet was able to thank God for His blessings and ask for help for me. The team arrived with Rebecca. They placed her in my arms. She smelled so wonderful and felt so good. I dressed her in a light blue, hand-smocked nightie I had made for her and hugged her. We all looked at her as the doctor stopped the respirator.

"Open your eyes, darling. Breathe, please breathe on your own." But there were no miracles, no eyes flickering open, no respiration. She did not suddenly look around and smile. Or did she? In those very moments — so sad for us — our dear little daughter was smiling on a world far brighter than she would have known here. She went from the safe shelter of the womb to the splendors of glory, hardly stopping here. She did not know sorrow or pain in this world of disappointment and limitations, only happiness and peace forever.

I raised her over my shoulder, feeling her soft head against my cheek. The ache was crushing. How I wanted her! Everything within my being wanted to cry out, "This can't be happening." Instead, I sat semi-composed and handed her body to the nurse. Rebecca was gone.

That night as I lay awake, unable to sleep, the words of a hymn came to me.

> *"What was it, O our God, led Thee to give Thy Son,*
> *To yield Thy well-beloved for us, by sin undone?*
> *Twas love unbounded led Thee thus*
> *To give Thy well-beloved for us."*

It was incomprehensible. *Give* His Son? To die? My baby was gone and I would not have given her for any reason. She was a baby I hardly knew while the Son of God, the Lord Jesus, had been with His Father eternally, in perfect fellowship and unity. Yet God gave His Son for me. Incredible! It was indeed "love unbounded." As I lay there in the quiet I wrote a little poem to Rebecca. It helped me to put her death in the proper perspective, as well as to say goodbye.

On Sunday, Mother's Day, I was discharged from the hospital. It was the day of Rebecca's funeral. It was nice to be home. We all needed each other and the sense of normalcy that being together brings.

At first, Jason did not want to go to the funeral. Then he decided that he would go since every one else was attending, but he was not comfortable with the idea. He found a job as doorman and was pleased to have something to do. We had decided on a small funeral asking only family, and friends from the Gospel Hall. Rebecca looked like a china doll in a bassinet, all pink and white and lovely. The service was brief, with Jon Procopio reading from II Samuel 12 and Dale reading the hymn "Under His Wings." We gathered our family around Rebecca for one last look. I kissed her cold little nose and turned to leave. The words of the poem I had written and pinned to the quilt in her casket rang in my ears...

For months we've been together
Every moment of each day
And always I have loved you
Just as I do today
I waited long to hold you
To hear your first sweet cry
To wrap my heart around you
Yet soft and still you lie
Had you only stayed awhile
We might have had such fun
Yet today I let you go
Dear precious little one
My Father in his wisdom
Has taken you above
And heaven is much nearer
Since you are there, my love

CHAPTER FOURTEEN

UNPREPARED

The children were saddened by Rebecca's death. MaryEllen was especially disappointed. She had looked forward to having a baby.

"You lied, Mommy," she said one day as she looked through the drawers in the nursery. "You said Rebecca would wear these clothes and she never wore a single one."

We had many discussions about heaven and how Rebecca was happier there than she would have been here. As we prayed with the children before bed Wes always thanked God for her place in His presence. That helped us all remember that knowing where we will spend eternity is what really matters. In a coming day, it will not make any difference that Rebecca reached heaven before the rest of us.

Jason dealt with the loss of his baby sister remarkably well. At first I was concerned that he might be internalizing his true feelings. Slowly I began to realize that he had a better grasp of life and death than I did. One night as he and Bryan were talking Bryan was lamenting the fact that Rebecca died.

Jason said, "It's not that sad. She's in heaven."

He knew what mattered! Jason had seen friends die. Those that he knew well and cared for had gone. This was a baby that he had never known. It was enough to know that he would meet her in heaven.

If only it had been that easy for me. The emptiness I felt is almost impossible to describe. There was also a strange sense of this whole tragedy being a kind of rehearsal. As morbid as it sounds, I had found myself wondering many times about Jason's possible death and what it would be like for Wes and me to have a funeral for a child we loved. Now I knew. I also found out that life goes on after we leave the fresh grave. How I resented that fact!

While my recovery was slow Jason was his happy self. He had all sorts of plans for the summer. He went off to Pittsburgh to visit his aunts and uncles, then on to Philadelphia to visit his dear friends, the Olivers. His illness and treatment rarely affected his love of life and his good nature.

One of his favorite pastimes was to go for long walks with Wes at night. The bond between them seemed to deepen even more. Knowing Jason's life might be shortened by the disease he was fighting, Wes made a point of pouring spiritual truths into Jason's young heart, stressing what a privilege it was to live each day for the glory of God. They had wonderful talks as they walked along, hand in hand, through downtown Saugus. More than simply having a father and son relationship, they became best friends.

Months passed relatively uneventfully, until an entire year had come and gone since Rebecca had so briefly visited our world. Just as the summer of 1990 began, a beautiful little blessing named

Sarah Elizabeth was born into our family and stole our hearts. She thrilled us all and was a tremendous help in recovering from the previous year's disappointment. When school began again Jason was a fifth grader. This would be his last year in elementary school. It seemed like only yesterday he had been a baby the size of Sarah. Where had the time gone?

Jason loved the fifth grade. There is something enjoyable about being one of the big kids and being looked up to by the younger students. He already was talking about the end of the year festivities. The class would go on special outings, swim at the YMCA and have a pizza party. Nearly every day he'd tell us about something special that made the year exciting. He was working hard, earning excellent grades and feeling well. December would mark three years of chemotherapy. We all looked forward to the treatment's being discontinued.

On December 6th Jason stayed home from school with a cold. During the day he seemed to improve so that by evening he was feeling fine. As he was getting ready for bed his nose started bleeding and did not stop easily. He told me he had two other nosebleeds earlier in the day. This wasn't very unusual, as Jason did tend to have nosebleeds with colds and congestion, or simply from the house being drier than usual with the heat on. As Jason and I were trying to get the bleeding under control, Wes came in from a meeting. He thought he should take Jason to the emergency room to have his blood counts checked. We phoned the doctor on call and she agreed. By that time it was 10 P.M.

At about 1 A.M. I awoke, surprised to find that Wes and Jason were still not home. Shortly afterward, Wes called to say they were having trouble getting blood as the port-a-cath was not working properly and veins were difficult to access. Knowing they would not be home for quite awhile, I went back to sleep.

Meanwhile, Wes was with Jason and he was the first to learn the shocking news.

The doctor examined Jason and then spoke to Wes: "I'm sorry, Wes, but the leukemia is back and he has between two weeks and two months to live."

Wes was stunned. After years of chemotherapy, the transplant and medications, was the end to be so sudden? Years before, Wes and Jason had made a promise to each other that Jason would try to bravely face whatever came and Wes, on his part, would be honest with Jason about his condition. Wes went to Jason and said, "Come on, buddy, let's go home."

Surprised, Jason asked, "What did they say?"

"Let's just go," Wes answered, his voice trembling with emotion.

As they went through the large front doors of Mass General Hospital Wes got down on his knees and said, "Oh, Jason, I love you so much, but your leukemia's back and it's all through you. The doctor just said you have only a few weeks or months to live."

He looked at Wes and his first words were, "Dad, this is going to be so hard on Mom ."

They walked to the car in silence. When finally they spoke, Jason wasn't angry or upset. He was thinking of how God might be able to use his death for a purpose, and he was determined to be the one to tell me the news.

Wes asked, "Jason, are you afraid?"

"No, Dad, I'm not afraid. I'm sorry for the family that this is happening."

Through tears, Wes told him, "Don't be sorry for us. Let's just do what we can, stick together, and see what God can work out of it." They prayed there at the end of the street and headed for home.

Of course, I knew nothing about this or of the nightmare through which Wes and Jason were passing. At about 3 A.M. I sensed someone in the hallway. I woke up to see Wes and Jason. Their expressions chilled me.

Wes looked at Jason and said, "Are you sure you want to tell her?"

"What?! Tell me what?" Jason came over to my side of the bed and knelt down on the floor. "My leukemia came back and they told me I have between two weeks and three months to live if I don't get chemotherapy," he said shakily.

I started to shiver. From head to toe my body shook with a dreadful chill. I hugged him to me, rocking him back and forth.

"Oh, my poor baby!"

It had been many years since I had called him "baby" but I only wanted to take him in my arms and shelter him from all this pain and grief. Wes asked him a little while later if there was anyone he wanted to talk to. Jason thought for a minute and then said he needed to call Jacki and Joey. They had been involved with Jason and his disease since the beginning. So, at 3:30 in the morning they once again received news neither will ever forget.

When we finally went to bed Jason was the only one who slept. Wes and I were in shock. Yes, we had realized this day would probably come, but again we were taken by surprise and unprepared. I remembered having said to a friend just the weekend before that I fully expected to lose Jason one day. We had been talking about her little girl who had died that summer, and my Rebecca. Never did I think that this would come so soon. We are never ready to lose someone we love.

The following day we returned to the hospital for further testing. Jason's regular doctor was almost as surprised as we were and was not convinced the diagnosis was correct. A bone marrow biopsy and aspiration were done, as well as more blood work. When the doctors looked at the bone marrow they felt very encouraged. It was not full of leukemia as should have been the case. The consensus was that either Jason was fighting off a virus or he had a chronic form of leukemia that many people live with for a long time. Bone marrow samples were sent to other labs for further study.

We left Mass General Hospital that day greatly relieved and hopeful. We would come back on Monday for more blood counts. The bad news had traveled fast and now we needed to let everyone know what the doctors had said. The excitement was contagious. Teachers were stopping by the house to hug Jason and to say what a miracle this was and an answer to all the prayers that had been said for Jason. I was cautiously optimistic. I had seen how this enemy called leukemia worked, sneaking up so slowly, then exploding into disaster. I had no doubt that God was able to answer our prayers and heal Jason, but we wanted only His will and were not sure what that will was. If Jason only had a virus why was he so pale? We could only hope for the best and go on from here. Today Jason was with us and we would enjoy that.

Over the next week Jason returned to the hospital several times for more blood work. The lab reports were still inconclusive. We grew more and more concerned as Jason was not feeling better or recovering from this possible "virus." Finally it was necessary to give him platelets due to his low platelet count and a white count that seemed to be going higher every day. On Monday, December 17th, I took Jason back for more tests and more platelets. I had an increasingly uneasy feeling while waiting to talk to the doctors. All the nurses seemed to avoid my impatient glances in their direction. When, at last, I was called into the office, I did not anticipate good news.

The doctor began, "Well, we are very concerned. This does not appear to be getting better. It is unreasonable to assume that this is a virus or a chronic form of leukemia. Jason appears to be in what we would describe as a blast crisis in AML (acute myelogenous leukemia). His white count is approaching dangerously high numbers and his platelets are being eaten up very rapidly."

I interrupted to ask what his white count was. When I was told it was nearly 200 thousand I was stunned. It had gone from 49,000 on December 6 to this incredible figure in just 11 days.

The doctor continued, "This does not appear to be a relapse of Acute Lymphocytic Leukemia because the disease seems to be in the transplanted marrow, not in his original marrow. If this had happened earlier there would be reason to question MaryEllen's health but, after five years, the possibility of the disease's coming from her is remote. More than likely the three years of chemotherapy are to blame for this new disease."

As I listened I became less concerned with where it came from and more interested in what we were to do about it. We seemed to go around in circles for a while. There was talk of possible aggressive treatments of chemotherapy and of second transplants. I felt we were skirting the real issue.

I finally spoke up, "Jason is not going to get better. He is going to die."

The doctor lowered his eyes. "Yes, no matter what we do, we are only putting off the inevitable."

Monica held my hand and suddenly seemed to be older and defeated. During more than 25 years she had known this defeat over and over again. Jason had been one of the "success" stories.

"We thought we had it licked," she said softly. "I'm getting too old for this."

I shared with her that I remembered asking Dr. Truman why he remained in such a field for so long. He had told me that he concentrated on the successes. She said that was true, if only every story had a happy ending. We talked about how long Jason might have. I wanted to pin someone down to a time, but everyone I asked said there was no way to predict. He could have weeks, perhaps months. So much depended on how well he did with whatever medication they could give him.

I told Monica that I did not want Jason to die at home. I could not imagine what that would be like for the other children. She said that was fine, that we could make those choices when the time came. Nonetheless, I realized that I might not have that choice should something happen suddenly.

Jason came into the office and Dr. Ferguson explained to him what was wrong. He asked if Jason had any questions. He didn't. They talked about chemotherapy. Jason said he would try some drugs but he did not want to be real sick if they were not going to make him better anyway. They seemed to understand each other. We decided to talk more about it later.

The ride home was quiet. Between the two of us there always had been a quiet understanding. We did not need to chatter much. Each of us knew, almost instinctively, what the other felt. I asked him what he was thinking. He sighed and said he was not surprised by what the doctor had said. I had not been either.

"Well it wasn't the best of news, for sure, and it sounds like it's probably not going to go away."

He said, "I know and that's okay."

In a few minutes he fell asleep and slept the rest of the way home. My mind was reeling. How do you tell your son that he is not going to get better? Yet, he did not need to be told — he knew.

CHAPTER **FIFTEEN**

A TENDER MESSAGE

Getting Jason through the holidays feeling relatively well became our main objective. He started on chemotherapy in pill form to get his white count down and a second medication to prevent bleeding. Transfusions were needed every few days even with this drug.

On Sunday, December 23rd, Jason had another bad nosebleed that required a trip to the emergency room for platelets. We were afraid he'd be admitted and unable to spend Christmas with us at home, but he responded to the treatment. We were on our way home in a few hours. Later that evening Becky and Dale arrived from Pennsylvania with their family, and others stopped by. Jason, feeling better, was delighted with all the visitors and quite talkative.

"I feel bad that everyone is so sad. People hug me and turn

away with tears in their eyes. Why is everybody so upset? They talk about how great it is to know you are going to heaven but when they find out you are really going — and going soon — they feel bad. It's not sad!"

"Jason," I said, "You are absolutely right, but think if it were the other way around. We are all thinking of how much we will miss you."

"Yeah," he said, "I guess so. I just wish people wouldn't cry or feel sorry for me. It makes me feel bad."

We all sat quietly. How could he possess such incredible strength and calm acceptance. He was not worried at all! "Great is thy faith" was all that kept coming before me.

In answer to many prayers, Jason enjoyed Christmas. He had a ride in a neighbor's Lambourghini — a real thrill — spent a nice day with his grandparents, aunts, uncles and cousins, and was feeling fabulous. We spent the afternoon playing games and enjoying each other. Over the next week Jason returned to the hospital for platelets several times but felt well enough to remain at home. The visiting relatives went home at the end of the week, not knowing if they would ever see Jason again. He understood and hugged them good-bye with great feeling.

Then he was on to the next project at hand. On Sunday December 30th, he was going to speak to the congregation at the Gospel Hall. He spent a lot of time thinking about what he wanted to say. Saturday evening he came into our bedroom to ask if he could have everyone sing after he spoke.

"I found this hymn I really like, Mom. I really want to sing it."

Just before Sunday School the next day Jason took the platform. He pulled a stool over, stood on it behind the podium and began to speak:

"If there's anyone here that doesn't know me my name is Jason Vitale. I'm here today to thank all the Christians who prayed for me and

helped with all the problems with my medical things. I also want to talk to the younger people here and say that there's an issue here that's very important. The Lord gives us a gift called salvation and it's most important that when we're young and in early ages we take the opportunity and get it settled. I know one thing that if I wasn't saved and didn't have the Lord's salvation from when I was just five years old that I probably wouldn't have been able to go through my operation and sickness the way I've done. He's helped me and He's always a Friend in troubles and any time we might be in pain or agony. If we're all by ourselves in a radiation room or during an operation or anything we can always know that the Lord's with us. He's a Friend that will never leave us and it's very important to get to know Him while you're young and not to despise the issue. You should hurry up with this and not fool around with the subject and say that today I'll do what I like to do with my sports and hobbies and I'll leave salvation till tomorrow because it's important and at any time in our life, especially at the end of life for older people and for younger people too. It's important not to say that only old people die because anyone can die at any age. It's up to the Lord. It's all in His hands obviously. I think we should make sure that we're not passing it by or letting it slip through our fingers. We all know, even the youngest people here know that the world's not looking very bright and it's probably not going to get much brighter. So I hope that you all don't despise what the Lord's trying to speak to you through. It might just be earthquakes or stories of people getting killed by car accidents and things. He's trying to tell everybody in the world that they can't fool around. It might be them someday and if it is He'd hate to see their soul crash out into a horror-struck eternity where there's no hope. That's why hundreds of years ago He sent His Son to die on the cross so that we might have a place in heaven. I hope that from the youngest to the oldest person here makes sure they don't despise this opportunity and makes sure they take the Lord's salvation. Thanks a lot to all the Christians for their help to me. They've really been ummm ....It's really something to know you have so many friends. Thanks a lot."

Then we sang — or tried to sing — Jason's favorite hymn:

"I have a home above from sin and sorrow free.
A mansion which eternal love designed and built for me.
My Father's gracious hand has built this blest abode;
From everlasting it was planned, my dwelling place with God.
My Savior's precious blood has made my title sure.
He passed through death's dark raging flood to make my rest secure.
The Comforter is come, the earnest has been given
He leads me onward to the home reserved for me in heaven.
Loved ones are gone before whose pilgrim days are done;
I soon shall greet them on that shore where partings are unknown.
But more than all, I long His glories to behold,
Whose smile fills all that radiant throng with ecstasy untold.
That bright, yet tender, smile, my sweetest welcome there,
Shall cheer me through the 'little while' I tarry for Him here.
Thy love, most gracious Lord, my joy and strength shall be,
Till Thou shalt speak the gladdening word that bids me rise to Thee.
And then, through endless days where all Thy glories shine,
In happier, holier strains I'll praise the grace that made me Thine."

No one made it through that hymn without breaking down.
The reality of Jason's words and the absolute peace in his manner as
he talked about death left even the children aware that they had
heard something very, very special. For his part, Jason was glad that
he had been able to express what he felt, and pleased to have it behind him. We went home to a seafood dinner he had requested.
Looking at him eating shrimp and smiling, one would never dream
he was so ill.

CHAPTER SIXTEEN

LETTING GO

New Year's day found Jason enjoying time with his good friends Eric, Dustin and Sean. They were able to race cars, play games and just have fun with each other. However, Jason's nose bled a lot and he was showing signs of weakness. The following day he was readmitted to the hospital after a reaction to platelets resulted in a high fever. We had lengthy discussions with the doctors as to what course of treatment to pursue. The transplant team at City of Hope was willing to try a second transplant if Jason's condition stabilized. Everything seemed to be very "iffy" at best.

We decided to consult Jason himself. As soon as we mentioned a second transplant he began to shake his head. Personally, I did not blame him. When we had watched him suffer so intensely I had silently vowed never to put him through that again. Wes, too, understood that medical science could only go so far. Ultimately, Jason was still in the Lord's hands. It seemed to us both that we had reached the end. Wes told the doctors that we would do what Jason wanted.

"We don't believe that quality of life is measured in quantity of days," Wes told them.

They understood and agreed that Jason's opinion was most important. Jason was only eleven years old, yet he was capable of this critical decision.

"No," he said softly, lying back on the pillow, "I don't want another transplant. I'll try some chemotherapy if it won't make me real sick. I just know I won't live through another transplant. I don't want to go through that for nothing."

"Jason," the doctor explained, "You don't have to decide that now. We need to try some medicine first to see if we can get that white count down some."

Jason had been given so many drugs over the years that few were left untried. Over the next few days he received doses of a new chemotherapy. As the deep blue medicine would slowly course into a vein in his hand I'd sit wondering what this poison would do to my son. He'd wince every now and then, complaining that the drug stung his arm. He missed his port-a-cath, which had recently been removed.

The days passed. Jason was disappointed that he was still in the hospital when his Uncle Pete arrived for a week's visit on the 10th. But four days later Jason came home. Delighted to be free while Pete was still around, Jason lost no time in dragging him off to MVP Sports for the all-important purchase of a knife to add to his collection. So when David and Melody Oliver arrived that afternoon from Philadelphia, expecting to find Jason lying on the couch, they weren't at all disappointed to have to wait for him to return from shopping. The excitement was short-lived, however, for the next day he was readmitted, following a particularly violent reaction to platelets. The effects of the chemotherapy were beginning to appear as well. His white count had plummeted to 400. Exhausted from the medication given to reduce the reaction and with his temperature soaring, Jason seemed to be wearing out from all the ups and downs he was experiencing. We felt it was so unfair that he should have to go through so much but he did not complain or bemoan his condition. The calmness he maintained was nothing short of miraculous.

One night, when he was having a particularly violent reaction to the platelets, a nurse was sent racing to the emergency room for medication. Wes stood on Jason's left, holding his hand, and Dr. Ferguson stood on his right.

Jason turned his head away from them, over his shoulder, toward the window, and whispered, "Help me, help me!"

Dr. Ferguson said, "Jason, I am trying to help you."

Jason looked up at him and said, "I wasn't asking for your help. I was asking for God's help."

Over the next several days Jason appeared to be slipping. His nose was constantly bleeding; his lips cracked and bled, making speaking and eating impossible. Both eyes became infected, requiring greasy ointment, which made his appearance all the more depressing. He wanted to come home but some new symptom would develop, making that impossible. Finally, on January 19th, Jason was discharged.

The next day Pete was to return to Pittsburgh. As he packed, I became aware of whispering and suspicious glances in my direction. When at last I was let in on the goings-on I was shocked. Jason was trying to convince Peter to take him to Pittsburgh with him. He could not be serious! This desperately ill child was thinking of travelling 600 miles. Quite a discussion followed. The reason Jason wanted to go to Pennslyvania was to talk to his friend Ronnie about salvation. Jason and Ronnie had been long distance friends ever since they could remember. As Jason thought about dying, it bothered him to think that Ronnie did not share his assurance of heaven.

"Dad, I really want to talk to him one more time."

While we hated the thought of Jason going away I had to understand and respect his wishes.

Finally we decided to call the doctor and go with his decision. Wes put in a call to the answering service. Within seconds the phone rang.

"Hello," Wes answered . "Oh, hello, Tom. It's funny you should call now. We were just waiting for the Doctor to return our call."

He went on to explain what we were waiting to find out and why. In minutes he hung up and returned to the living room shaking his head. Apparently Uncle Tom, in Pittsburgh, had been thinking along the same lines and wanted to fly Jason there or come to Boston himself. This couldn't be a coincidence.

Jason smiled and said, "See, the Lord heard me!"

When the doctor called he agreed the decision was Jason's. The worst that could happen was that he would die. Death was coming eventually, wasn't it? As nervous as I was about this whole issue I backed off and let Jason decide what he wanted to do.

"If I go there I can see more people than if they come here, so I think I should go. I know you don't want me to leave but I think that if God can get me there in such an amazing way He'll bring me back too." Then he asked, "Do you want to come with me, instead of Daddy?"

After thinking it over I decided not to go. Sarah was only six months old and still nursing. I felt it would be impossible to leave her and knew I was not capable of managing a baby and a critically ill child on a plane. Wes and Jason left the following morning, while it was still dark. As I helped him dress I noticed the changes this disease called leukemia had made in my son. He was so thin and pale. Nearly twelve years old now he looked more like an elderly man. As I crawled back into bed I prayed that God would allow me to see him again the following afternoon.

The next day, we watched for the familiar car to come up the road. The flight had been delayed due to bad weather and I had grown more anxious with each passing hour. Finally they were coming!

Then Jason was in my arms, smiling and saying, "See, Mom, I told you God would bring me home!"

As weak as he was, he was thrilled he had been able to make the trip. It was worth all the anxiety on our part, just to see his happiness. Jason lay on the couch and said he planned to stay there. As Wes and I discussed the trip later I was again very thankful to the Lord for bringing my little boy home to me. I did not realize how worried Wes had been that Jason would not make it home. For the hour or so before their flight home, Jason had been blacking out and feeling tremendously weak. Jason, not at all fearful, had leaned back in his seat on the plane, smiling. He had accomplished what he felt God had wanted him to do. He had been able to talk to Ronnie and say his good-byes.

"Dad, I'm really ready to go now."

Wes knew he needed platelets badly but there was no way to get them, and he just prayed that Jason would make it home.

The very next day Jason was due at Mass General Hospital for the usual platelets. I dressed to take him and was encouraging him to get ready when he appeared in the doorway of our room.

"Mom, I'm not going to the hospital today." I turned around, surprised.

"Okay," I finally said. "Maybe you will feel like it tomorrow."

"Mom, I'm not going tomorrow either. I don't want any more platelets because they aren't doing any good. I get sicker and sicker every time and then I have to stay there."

I took a deep breath. Was this happening? I wanted to argue,

"No, we have to go. The doctors want us to come. This is what we're supposed to do," but I could not. Jason was right. We were fooling ourselves if we believed he was improving or stabilizing towards another transplant. It was not going to happen. We had witnessed the slow defeat of other children too often to mistake what was happening to our son. Jason was dying and there was nothing we could do to stop it from happening.

How I hated this realization. This was not supposed to happen! We grow up expecting to lose grandparents and, perhaps, our parents on some far away day. But this was my little boy. I had given birth to him, held him, loved him unreservedly. While we had lived for seven years with the possibility of losing him, the sense of helplessness I was feeling at that moment was overwhelming.

I called the hospital and spoke with Monica. She assured me that Jason's decision was very adult and perfectly acceptable. She advised us to accept the aid of a visiting nurse. She also explained to me some of the things we might expect. I asked her how long Jason had. Again no one could say for certain. It could be a few days if he experienced internal head bleeding. Then again, he might last for several weeks.

Later that day, Laurie, a visiting nurse, stopped by. She explained to us that Jason would probably sleep more and more until he died. We were to call her and she would take care of everything. We wouldn't need to contact the police or emergency crews, but she suggested we contact the funeral home soon.

Once more we found ourselves in the office of the young funeral director who had endeared himself to us by his handling of Rebecca's funeral. We were impressed by the care and sympathy he had shown. He was obviously upset as we discussed plans. He remembered Jason as the doorman at Rebecca's funeral; it seemed incomprehensible to him that we were there to make arrangements for Jason's. We decided it would be best to have both the viewing and the funeral at the Walnut St. Gospel Hall.

As we prepared to leave he said, "I hope I don't hear from you for a long time."

Our house was constantly filled with friends and relatives. Jason loved visiting with everyone. Each afternoon the teachers came from the Oaklandvale School, the one our children attend. Neighbors and friends brought Jason cards, toys and homemade cookies. It was a bit overwhelming to be the objects of such loving support. Whatever we needed was there before we had time to think about it.

Jon Procopio had arrived from Labrador, where he preaches the gospel. He knew Jason was losing ground rapidly and wanted to spend some time with him before he died. Jason was thrilled to have him around. We cannot imagine what we would have done without him. Jon was there for Jason to talk to. He provided an extra pair of hands to hold a glass of water, fix a blanket, or help one of the other children. Just knowing he was around made us feel better. Thinking of the 2000 miles he had traveled, and of his wife and family braving the wild weather of the North without him made us even more appreciative.

Wes was unable to work. It had become increasingly difficult for him to fulfill his responsibilities and at the same time run to Jason's aid when necessary. His boss is a wonderful man who could not have been more understanding or helpful. The children continued to go to school each day but, other than that, all sense of routine and organization was gone.

Jason was taking morphine in small amounts. He had begun to get restless and complain of pain in his legs. He was steadily weakening but was not in excruciating pain or suffering terribly. He enjoyed all the company he had and would constantly think of things to do to involve everyone. Some days he wanted to play a game. One day he decided we were going to build Legos. He had enjoyed many hours of constructing with Legos in the long hospital stay in California. This particular day he decided he wanted a new set. Wes and Jon scoured the town in search of "Eldorado Fortress." He was so concerned they get the right thing that he got up and searched for the book that showed it. We smiled as he scurried around. He was indeed a child after all. For days he had lain there so ill and then, for the sake of a toy.... He lit up as they returned with the precious box. Then he lay on the couch giving instructions as I assembled it with help from the children and those who dropped by.

Because Jason refused to go upstairs to bed, Wes started camping out in the living room. We were afraid to leave him. One night, however he decided to sleep in the girls' bedroom when they were away. Early in the morning Wes went into the room. "Okay, I'll see you. Thanks for coming" Jason said. Wes asked what he meant.

"Oh I was just saying good-bye to Dan's wife."

"Jason, she wasn't here."

"I know, Dad, but I see people in my head. When I die if any one says they are sorry they didn't come to see me, tell them that's okay. I saw them anyway."

Wes's mouth dropped. They lay there hugging quietly. Wes broke the silence, "You know, Jason, when you die I won't just be losing a son, I'll be losing my best friend."

"Dad?"

"Yes, Jason."

"Are you afraid of waking one morning and finding me dead?"

Wes gulped, "Well, you don't beat around the bush. Yes, I guess I am."

"Dad, I'll tell you what. If I think I know when it's going to happen I'll try to give you a sign."

"Okay, Bud, I love you."

In the wee hours of January 29th Wes woke me up. "You should come downstairs. Jason's acting strange."

Hurriedly, I followed him to where Jason was. We gave him

142

a big drink of water and some medicine. He seemed to settle down so I kissed him good night and went back to bed. Several hours later I went downstairs to find him still asleep. Wes got up, the children went off to school, I bathed and dressed Sarah, and still Jason slept. We were not too worried, since he had been up so much during the night and was probably tired. Eventually he stirred and acted a bit confused. Was he thirsty? As the glass was held to his lips his head rolled back. He was unable to hold it up. The water ran out of his mouth and he was asleep again. We all looked at each other rather blankly. This was not a bad dream; we were losing Jason. For most of the day he continued to sleep. People came and went throughout the afternoon. Occasionally he roused himself enough to acknowledge a visitor, but most of the time they would speak to him, not knowing whether he heard them or not. It was very touching to watch friends kneeling beside the couch, speaking softly in his ear. I chose to believe that he heard every word. After all, he heard his dad crying as Wes sat looking at him on the couch.

He asked softly, "Who is crying?"

Wes crept to his side and hugged him.

Jason placed his hand on his father's head and said, "Don't cry for me."

He fell back to sleep. A short while later Jason pointed to the ceiling. At first we all thought he wanted to interrupt the conversation that was going on nearby. However, he never tried to say a word. The sign! He had promised Wes he would try to signify when the end was near. That must have been what he was trying to tell us. Did he think he was dying?

That evening was the prayer meeting night at the Walnut Street Gospel Hall. Instead of going, Joey and Jon Procopio came to sit with us. Wes and I decided to sleep in shifts. He went to bed with the children. When I went up at midnight he arose. Jason was still sleeping. I found it hard to relax and went back downstairs. For two hours I sat watching Jason as he peacefully slept. Every now and then one of us would check his pulse. We noticed his feet and legs were very cold. The others kept telling me to return to bed. I finally decided to listen to them. Before I left I laid my head next to Jason's. After a minute or two I stood up and started to leave.

Jason turned his head and asked, "What happened?"

His eyes were wide, almost as though he were forcing them to remain open. He mumbled a few words that we could not understand, then said clearly, "Tell her I saw the Lord."

That was a message for Grammy Vitale. A few days earlier Jason had heard her singing "Face to Face with Christ My Savior." Shortly after that he began to wave his arms around. It frightened us, as we thought he was struggling to breathe.

Jon looked at him intently. "I think he wants to hug you" he said.

Quickly I moved to sit on the edge of the couch and leaned over him. Jason reached his arms up around my neck and squeezed. He then pulled back slightly, put one hand to his face and pinched his cheeks together to enable his mouth to form a kiss. He repeated the process, meaning it for Wes, but could not quite reach him. He seemed to drift back into unconsciousness and then said,

"Life's tough."

Joe replied, "Life's tough but heaven is better, right, Jay?"

With the slightest hint of a smile, he answered, "Uh-huh."

Gradually, his breathing slowed and his pulse faded.

"He's going now," Jon said. Speaking softly to Jason, telling him he'd awaken in heaven, Jon put his hand on Jason's neck, feeling the weak throb subside.

Jason was gone.

Now I could hug him and not worry about hurting him. Holding him to me, I sobbed my good-bye. Wes saw instantly that all that had been Jason, all that he loved about him was actually gone, transported to another world. Jason's body lay there peacefully but the real Jason, his soul, was in heaven. It was over. Life with its pain and sorrow had ended for Jason. While we were looking at him with sadness, his spirit was entering the magnificent splendor of heaven. We knew he was perfectly at home there. Suddenly it seemed so right that he should be with the Lord he loved so dearly.

CHAPTER **SEVENTEEN**

UNTIL THEN

Jason would have liked his funeral. Hundreds came to say their good byes to a little boy who had touched them in an unforgettable way. Those who spoke at the funeral would have embarrassed him by speaking of him so highly. However, he would have been delighted to hear them speak so well of his Savior. Jason wanted his friends to hear the clear message of the gospel. Many people knew that Jason was a Christian and had seen tremendous faith in his life. But perhaps they never had heard the wonderful news that the Lord Jesus loved them and died to put their sins away and secure a place in heaven for them. In a clear and memorable manner, those who spoke at the funeral reminded the audience of these great truths and of their power in Jason's life.

It was difficult to look into that angelic, boyish face for the last time. As I bent and kissed his now-cold nose my mind flashed back to the delivery room where I saw Jason Michael for the first time, then to a towheaded tot full of smiles and laughter as he carried his baby sister like a horse. Where had the years gone? How could we turn and walk away, leaving him?

In the days that followed, we found ourselves resenting the fact that life was moving on. The clocks kept ticking, the calendar pages turning, leaving us feeling like bystanders. We were seeing life happen but noticing little and feeling so alone and empty. How would we ever laugh or be happy again? Yet, how would Jason have wanted us to feel? Surely he would not want us to be continually sad. We made an effort to focus on the positive, the spiritual, and tried not to dwell on our loss.

Still, our world will never be the same. We are forever thankful to God for allowing Jason to touch our hearts. Through him we learned much about God's sustaining grace, love and power. While he taught us a lot about dying, he taught us much more about living as we witnessed a peace that comes from trusting God completely.

Often we remember the words of II Samuel 12:23: "*I shall go to him, but he shall not return unto me.*"

Jason once told us, "God puts us here and gives us a job to do. When it is done he takes us home to heaven. God is going to bless me by taking me home early. Do what you are supposed to do, raise your family for God and I'll see you when you get there (heaven)."

EPILOGUE

One day, while out walking, I saw three of Jason's former classmates. It was wonderful to see them, but I was amazed at how grown up they looked. How would Jason like being a teenager? It seemed odd that his friends had continued to grow and change. They, like Jason, were frozen in my mind as fifth graders.

I missed Jason. How could he be gone? When I closed my eyes I saw him laughing and joking with these friends as they walked along the sidewalk. He wore the same tan jacket and black sneakers, carried his books and listened to Ming telling a joke. Stacy and Jared looked on, smiling. Quickly, reality returned, and I found myself driving to the cemetery.

It had been a long time since I had been to his grave. The polished granite marker read — *Jason Vitale February 7, 1979-*

January 30, 1991 Home in heaven — Jesus died for me. Emptiness shook me. What had I expected to find here, after all? The words of the verse, *Why seek ye the living among the dead. He is not here...* echoed in my mind.I imagined Jason shaking his head as he watched his mother, standing alone in a cold cemetery; just because she wanted to be near him.

I thought of the warmth, brightness, and beauty of heaven. Jason was with the Lord. My emptiness vanished; I did not belong here. Looking upward, I smiled and blew Jason a kiss.

The three years since Jason's death have passed quickly. I know much good has come from our loss. Several people, including Ronnie — Jason's friend from Pennsylvania — have trusted in Christ as their personal Saviour. I would like to think that many others, unknown to us, have done the same. My parents, apart for fifteen years, were remarried.

At times, when missing Jason, I picture him here, a part of the chaos we call family life. He is holding Ashley — a sister he has never seen — or laughing at Sarah's antics, helping MaryEllen or Bryan with their schoolwork or teasing Bethany. It is nice to think that he is not missing us. And I am comforted by his words, "Life's tough, heaven is better."

PHOTO**ALBUM**

ABOVE: Jason with Bethany and Wes. **BELOW:** Day following his diagnosis at MGH

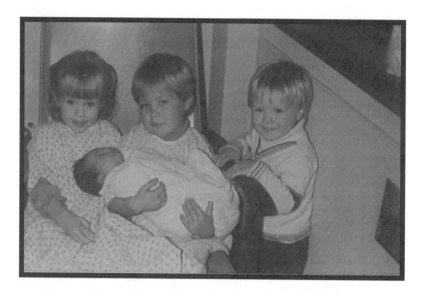

ABOVE: MaryEllen arrives. **BELOW:** Bethany, MaryEllen and Bryan tested as bone marrow donors.

ABOVE: MaryEllen is the donor. (Eagle Tribune Photo)

ABOVE: Leaving for California. **BELOW:** In isolation.

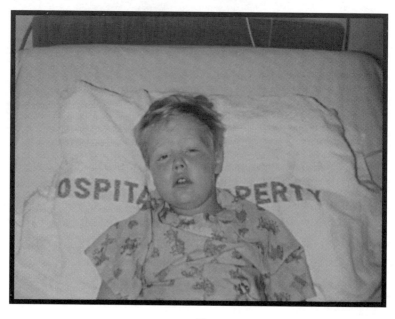

ABOVE: The walk in the rose garden— after which he slept and slept. **BELOW:** Jason and Eric together again.

ABOVE: Feeling well and growing hair. (Eagle Tribune Photo)

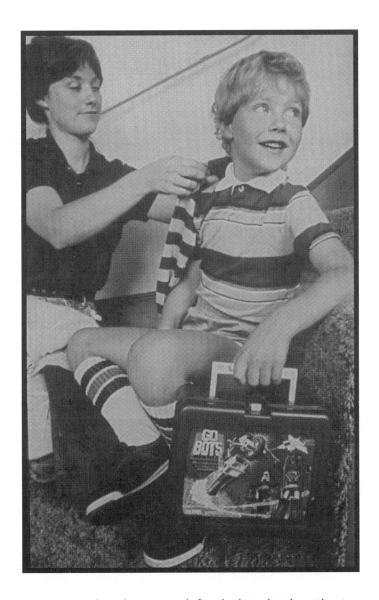

ABOVE: Martha with Jason— ready for school. (Eagle Tribune Photo)

ABOVE: Sick again. Family and Uncle Fred and Aunt Tre. **BELOW:** Enjoying his four wheeler.

ABOVE: Speaking at a Leukemia Society Event. **BELOW:** Admiring new sister Sarah.

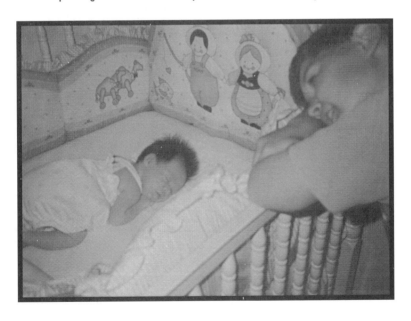

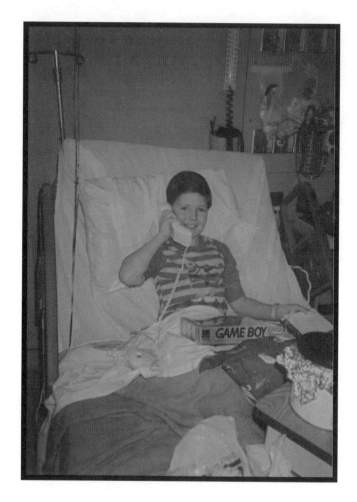

ABOVE: Back in the hospital.

ABOVE: With Lilian Guay— one of Jason's many friends.

ABOVE: Dinner following his speaking at the Gospel Hall. **BELOW:** A special friend—
Uncle Frank Procopio

ABOVE: In Pennsylvania with Ronnie. **BELOW:** Jason's last picture– with Jon Procopio

PHOTO BY: JuBINVILLE PHOTO